The Complete Book of

SPEECH COMMUNICATION

workbook of ideas and activities for students of speech and theatre

CAROL MARRS

Illustrated by Lafe Locke

MERIWETHER PUBLISHING LTD.
Colorado Springs, Colorado

Meriwether Publishing Ltd., Publisher
PO Box 7710
Colorado Springs, CO 80933-7710

Editor: Arthur L. Zapel
Cover and book design: Tom Myers
Illustrations by Lafe Locke

Library of Congress Cataloging-in-Publication Data

Marrs, Carol, 1955-
        The complete book of speech communication : a workbook of ideas
    and activities for students of speech and theatre / by Carol Marrs :
    illustrated by Lafe Locke.
            p.   cm.
        Includes bibliographical references.
        ISBN-13: 978-0-916260-87-3
        ISBN-10: 0-916260-87-9
        1. Public speaking. 2. Oral communication. 3. Acting--Study and
    teaching. 4. Drama. I. Title.
    PN4121.M3315 1992
    808.5--dc20   91-47621
                                                          CIP

6   7   8   07   08   09

Dedication

To Greg, Matthew and Haley

Acknowledgments

*A special thanks to Jean Hall for her help,
hard work, love and encouragement.*

*To the many dedicated and talented teachers I've known
who have contributed to the wealth of ideas within.*

*And to the many creative and enthusiastic students I've had
who continue to be a source of inspiration.*

Table of Contents

CHAPTER SIX

The Play's the Thing
Acting & Dramatics 65

Activities

CHAPTER SEVEN

Is That a Fact?
Researched Speeches 91

Activities

CHAPTER EIGHT

Instant Speech

CHAPTER NINE

Bring Literature to Life

CHAPTER TEN

Grab Bag

How to Use This Book

Instructions — The instructions for all the speech communication activities included in this book are set apart in boxes. These may easily be photocopied and posted or handed out so that each student understands the activity without wasting a lot of class time on the "how to." In some cases the boxed instructions are carried over onto the next page. The top and bottom of the box may simply be spliced together to make a complete box. The author and publisher permit this limited photocopying privilege without violation of the copyright. No other sections may be photocopied without permission.

Topic Suggestions — You will find lists of speech topic suggestions throughout this book. Although students certainly aren't limited to these ideas, they will be helpful for those who have a difficult time choosing a subject. Just for fun, you might try copying the topics on slips of paper. Students can draw out a topic when you "pass the hat." This can be a good way to promote the exploration of new subject matter.

You will find it helpful to use the Sign-Up Sheet on page 153 (accompanying explanation of form is on page 152) where students can list their chosen topics. This form will help to ensure that a wide variety of topics are chosen without duplication of topics.

Organization Outline — Pages 19 and 20 describe how to use an outline to organize a speech into logical sequence, from the introductory remarks to the conclusion. This basic structure may be adapted for all the various types of speeches in this book.

Terms to Learn — Vocabulary words are listed at the beginning of each chapter. Discussing their meaning is a good introductory activity to "kick off" each new chapter. By establishing the meaning of these words, you will set the tone for the rest of the chapter and promote better learning of the concepts and activities.

Grab Bag — These varied activities from Chapter Ten may be worked into the daily class periods as time permits, or you may opt to have "Grab Bag Days" where you experiment with these fun topics. The class may choose to present some of these grab bag activities to other students in a variety show setting. The "Entertainment" speech, the "Pet Peeve" speech, and Improvisational Theatre are all good candidates for a variety show.

Progress Reports — See page 151. This is a good activity for both students and teachers to evaluate where you've been and where you're going. Don't forget to do this at midterm, if not sooner. You'll discover what activities have worked the best and you will glean useful information for the remainder of the semester and speech communication classes to come.

Introduction

This text is designed to help develop the skills necessary to become an effective communicator. It is written for those who believe that students learn best by doing. If the "doing" can involve imaginative materials that stimulate creativity, then there will be an excitement and desire to learn. The text is designed to provide numerous activities that promote student participation and involvement. It offers vocabulary, objectives, lead-in information and activities for application. Each activity is fully explained and described in step-by-step detail so that teachers and students can easily know how to prepare and present the assignment.

The book has many activities that can be incorporated into a full-year's course in speech communication. It is a text which is both adaptable and flexible. Materials and activities may be easily added to or deleted from this text. The assignments will help students become more efficient, more self-confident, more creative and more successful as communicators.

The book is divided into ten chapters. Each chapter provides information which leads into certain activities. Chapter one deals with intrapersonal communication. Chapter two focuses on beginning speeches, especially visual aids speech topics. Chapter three allows for partner speeches while chapter four deals with reasoning speeches. Various types of storytelling techniques are emphasized in chapter five. Acting and dramatics are discussed in chapter six, chapter seven allows for speeches which require research and chapter eight discusses impromptu speaking. Chapter nine explores oral interpretation and chapter ten offers a grab bag of various speech activities.

Speech communication is the key to learning. Building strong communication skills can help us unlock the door to a better self-understanding. It can aid us in building stronger relationships as we develop greater ease in expressing our thoughts and feelings effectively and understandably.

Learning to have self-confidence, to listen carefully, to organize our ideas, to prepare and practice, to be aware of nonverbal messages and to continue to develop intrapersonally are only a few of the invaluable skills which can be achieved through a study in speech communications.

I hope this book provides the information and the activities needed to give a firm foundation in speech communication as it stimulates your interest and involves you in an enjoyable and rewarding learning experience.

CHAPTER ONE

Getting to Know Me

Intrapersonal and Interpersonal Communication

Terms to Learn

communication
intrapersonal communication
interpersonal communication
self-concept
self-esteem

interview
interviewer
interviewee
perception
stereotype

Communication is the process of sending and receiving messages to achieve understanding. It involves a sender, message, receiver and response. It can take place within ourselves or with those around us. The type of communiction which takes place within ourselves is called *intrapersonal communication.* Getting to know yourself is one of the most important goals in becoming a better communicator. Intrapersonal communication involves so many facets of your life, especially the way you communicate with others. This type of actual communication with one or more individuals is called *interpersonal communication.*

Development of our intrapersonal and interpersonal communication skills is vital to both our personal and professional lives. Both types of communication allow us to constantly analyze what we see, feel and

3

hear. We then form opinions, feelings, needs, likes, dislikes, strengths and weaknesses which make up the essence of our personalities. Our basic personality controls many activities in our lives. If we are shy, we stay to ourselves, unable to interact freely with others. If we are bold and confident, we tend to be more outgoing and can engage more freely in interpersonal communication.

Understanding who you are, how you see yourself, how others see you and how you wish for others to see you is essential in improving your self-concept. Your **self-concept** is your picture of yourself formed from personal beliefs, attitudes and experiences. Everything you have experienced in your life comes into play as your self-concept is formed. It encompasses the physical, intellectual, and social sides of your personality. Each of us has ideas of who and what we would like to be, but understanding and liking who we are at the present is vital if we are to move ahead toward that personal goal.

Realizing that no one personality type is superior to any other allows us to truly appreciate ourselves and others as individuals. Tuning in to our personality strengths and cultivating them will enable us to grow. Working to minimize our character weaknesses will also help to build a positive self-image. Once you accept who you are and where your strengths and weaknesses lie, you can be on the road to a self-understanding that allows you to achieve all that you desire.

Self-esteem is the opinion you have of yourself based on your personal self-concept. A high self-esteem can be created through positive remarks and reinforcement. The messages, sent by others, both verbal and nonverbal, cause us to react accordingly. Positive messages can make us feel very worthwhile while negative feedback can produce low self-esteem. With a positive self-concept and high self-esteem, you have the  confidence to try new things because you believe you have the ability to succeed. Believing you can succeed is the key to success.

Name Game

Starting a new class can be a frightening experience. Breaking the ice on Day One can make a big difference in the size of those first day jitters. Making new friends on the first day of class can leave a student with a secure, relaxed feeling. The Name Game helps a new group get acquainted while giving everyone in class a chance to speak. Those who are nervous can find a little peace with the fact that everyone will have to speak at some point during the first meeting. The game also promotes good listening skills because everyone must pay close attention to the information given, not knowing when their turn will come. The game is great for learning everyone's name as well as an interesting fact about each person.

It can be done two ways — by having names repeated, or names and personal facts recalled. Time and number of people will dictate which name game can be used. The Name Game is a great exercise for the teacher or leader as they get to know all members of their class. The teacher can put all participants at ease by telling them that he will be the last participant of the game and recall all names. The game is a fun first day challenge.

ACTIVITY — Name Game

O B J E C T I V E S

1. To stimulate memory through repetition.
2. To get to know all participants of a given group.
3. To recall names of class or group members.

I N S T R U C T I O N S

1. The first person states his name and something interesting about himself. You may want to fill in the blanks to this sentence. My name is _____ and I like _____.
The second blank could be a favorite food, sport, person, singing group or hobby.

2. The second person states his name and something about himself. Then he states the first person's name and the interesting fact, and so on. It gets harder and longer as the game progresses.

3. The game continues until each person has introduced himself.

4. Select participants at random to keep everyone on their toes. One way to do this is to allow number one to select number two and so

---

on. No one will know when his turn will come so all will remain active listeners.

5. To encourage those who have taken their turns to remain interested, give an incentive such as a bonus point for anyone who can name everyone at the end of the class meeting. Other things can be used as an incentive, depending on the class and situation.

The Personal Interview

With everyone acquainted in class, the interpersonal communication process can be taken a step further through personal interviewing. An **interview** is a formal kind of interpersonal communication involving two persons with a definite goal in mind, usually that of gaining information. The person being interviewed or questioned is the **interviewee,** and the Individual who presents the questions is the **interviewer.**

Knowing someone's name is just the beginning in establishing a relationship. Finding out their likes, dislikes, hopes, dreams and life goals provides the opportunity for friendships to be formed. Many similar factors are revealed through the interview. People find they have many things in common. It also allows for personal introspection as the interviewee must look deeply into his own personality to answer the questions asked by the interviewer.

ACTIVITY — The Personal Interview

O B J E C T I V E S

1. To get to know other class members.
2. To develop interviewing skills.
3. To allow students to learn something about themselves.

I N S T R U C T I O N S

1. Each student needs a partner.
2. Each student should devise a list of interesting questions leaving enough space to record answers.
3. Students should take turns asking their partners questions, completing the entire interview before changing roles. They will first be either an

interviewer or interviewee and then change positions with their partners.

4. Record all answers on paper.

5. Complete 10-15 questions or as many as time allows.

6. Students stand and tell several interesting things they learned about their partners, as the teacher calls on each student or as the students volunteer.

7. Each person will have the opportunity to speak and tell about the person they interviewed.

8. The teacher can emphasize how each student is different, yet many students have common answers and interests.

9. The teacher can also discuss how much easier it is to talk about someone else as compared to telling about ourselves.

The Personality Poem

As you get to know others, it is also very beneficial to get to know yourself. Continuing to discover the many different sides of your personality is a never-ending process. There are so many ways to understand who you actually are. One way is to ask yourself questions about your feelings. Who are you? What things do you like? What do you do well? An honest evaluation of self will be the first step in improving your self-concept.

ACTIVITY — The Personality Poem

OBJECTIVE

1. To learn more about yourself.

INSTRUCTIONS

1. Answer the following questions in writing. Who are you? I am
   _____. What are your likes and dislikes? I
   like _____. I dislike _____.
   What are some things you do well? They are _____.
   How do you think others see you? Others see me _____.

7

Why do they see you in this way? Because _____
_____. How do *you* see yourself? I see myself_____
_____.

2. These questions are designed to lead you into a personality poem.

3. Write your first name vertically or down the side of the paper (If your first name is short, use your first and last name).

4. Use each letter of your name to tell something about you that is a true fact.

5. Your poem may rhyme or be blank verse.

6. Now, share and tell about yourself.

Getting Acquainted

Another exercise which allows for intrapersonal growth is a getting acquainted with yourself writing assignment. All of us have dreams and desires about how we would like to be. Taller, shorter, smarter, funnier, more organized, more talkative, less sensitive, the list is endless. How do we achieve these dreams? How do we move closer to being that person we dream of being? One step at a time, that's how. We look at one weak area and concentrate on that one thing. We work on being proud of the many strengths we possess and at the same time zero in on the one thing that we want to change. Go ahead! Get acquainted with you!

ACTIVITY — Getting Acquainted

OBJECTIVE

1. To promote pride, self-concept and self-acceptance.

INSTRUCTIONS

1. Write a paragraph describing yourself.
2. Describe what you look like and how you dress.
3. Write things you like to do, things you dislike.
4. Write about your special talents, your shortcomings.
5. Does your description sound like someone you would like to know? Or someone you would rather avoid?
6. Write a second paragraph describing what you wish you could be.
7. How would you change yourself?
8. What abilities would you develop?
9. Compare what you are and what you would like to be.
10. What things can you do to bring the "wish" description closer to the "now" version?
11. This can be a private assignment or one that is shared with the class.

Individual Differences

Every person is unique. No two people enjoy the same things or act the same way. Your attitude toward the way you communicate affects everything you do. Your confidence level affects the way other people perceive you. **Perception** plays a vital role in the communication process. It is the reception and interpretation of stimuli that has to do with the five senses: sight, touch, taste, smell and hearing. Each of us has our own way of looking at things. Why we see things a certain way depends on our backgrounds, our experiences. It is essential that we learn to accept others no matter how different they may appear. We cannot allow ourselves to **stereotype**, or label people as part of a group and treat them as if they possessed only the characteristics of that group. We must accept people for who they are, realizing that we are all unique individuals.

ACTIVITY — Individual Differences

OBJECTIVE

1. To emphasize each person's uniqueness.

1. List in writing the many differences you observe among classmates.
2. Discuss the differences you observed.
3. The teacher should emphasize the fact that no two people are alike, and everyone is allowed to be who and what they choose to be.
4. This can be a short filler activity, or it can be a lengthy discussion about individuality.

Self-Awareness Personal Profile

Being able to fully understand ourselves, the important things we have experienced, the meaningful relationships we have, the way we see every aspect of our personalities can open our eyes to our capabilities. We have the power over our own lives. What we choose to do with that power is up to us.

ACTIVITY — Self-Awareness Personal Profile

OBJECTIVE

1. To promote personal self-awareness.

1. The student will create a folder which is a personal profile of him/herself.
2. The cover of the folder should be a personality collage which com-

pletely describes the student. Words, pictures, personal drawings, anything which helps to define who that person is.

3. In the first paper, the student will write several paragraphs in which he identifies himself. This should include likes, dislikes, prejudices, talents, personality traits, good and bad.

4. Next, the student will write another paper in which he analyzes himself socially, intellectually, emotionally, morally, religiously and economically.

5. The third paper will be about an event which the student considers to be very memorable.

6. The fourth paper will be about something, either abstract or concrete, which the student holds to be of value. Tell why it is important.

7. Fifth, the student will describe his family — telling about brothers, sisters, their ages, personalities, hobbies, occupations, and attitudes of the family members.

8. Last, the student will put together several pages of photograph pictures with captions. The pictures should tell the student's life story from birth to present.

9. An optional, but fun part of the assignment. The student will present the pictures with captions in an informal speech presentation. This presentation should include an introduction, body and conclusion.

Person I Would Most Like to Be

Having a clear image of the complete you will enable you to reach the personal goals you set for yourself. Very few people are completely satisfied about the way they are now. Working slowly and realistically toward the person you would like to become is a way to improve self-concept.

Do you ever dream of being someone else or like someone else? It could be a friend, family member or even a famous celebrity. It's fun to imagine what life would be like if you were someone else, especially when you are able to pick that person.

11

ACTIVITY — Person I Would Most Like to Be

O B J E C T I V E

1. To recognize the desirable qualities possessed by people we admire.

I N S T R U C T I O N S

1. Make a list of people you admire, look up to or idolize.
2. Choose one person that you would most like to be.
3. List all reasons why you would like to be that person.
4. Tell what you would do if you were that person.
5. Sum up the speech for your conclusion.
6. Be sure to think of all characteristics this person possesses that you like or admire.
7. This speech can be presented informally by having class members share portions of their speeches through discussion, or it may be presented as a formal speech.

Description of Best Friend (or family member)

As you develop your interpersonal communication skills, you cultivate relationships. You may become closer with a family member or form a new friendship. As you build upon that relationship, you learn more about that person. You learn what special qualities you like in that person. You share things with that person. You support him/her. You are a good listener, and you are there for that person. Above all, take time to "feed" that special relationship. It cannot exist without nurturing and special care.

ACTIVITY — Description of Best Friend (or family member)

O B J E C T I V E

1. To develop an understanding of friendship.

I N S T R U C T I O N S

1. Write a description of your best friend.
2. Your description should include a complete physical description of your best friend.
3. It should include all interests and hobbies of that person.

4. Most importantly, it should include the special traits which attracted you to that person — character traits which especially stand out in that person's personality.

5. You will not read your description. You will *tell* about the person, only occasionally referring to your notes.

Intrapersonal Inventory

We are indeed complex beings with our many sides. The process of communicating with ourselves is going on constantly. Even when we are not speaking to our inner-selves, we are thinking. We are exchanging ideas within ourselves. The way we think and feel today may be completely different tomorrow given a new situation or set of circumstances. Nevertheless, it's fun to get a clearer look at the you of today.

Here's a fun exercise in developing the intrapersonal process.

ACTIVITY — Intrapersonal Inventory

O B J E C T I V E
1. To develop intrapersonal communications.

I N S T R U C T I O N S

1. Ask yourself the questions below.

2. Don't be disturbed if you cannot easily put your exact responses into words.

3. Try as best as you can to express your answers so that you could communicate them to others if you so desired.

1. I like the color _____ because _____.

2. _____ is my best friend because _____.

3. My favorite food is _____ because _____.

4. I like the song _____ because _____.

5. My favorite holiday is _____ because _____.

6. My favorite class in school is _____ because _____.

7. _____ is my favorite movie because _____.

8. I want to travel to _____ because _____.

13

9. I usually worry about _____.

10. I get angry when _____.

11. I'm happiest whenever _____.

12. If I were an animal, I'd be a _____.

13. If I were a color, I'd be _____.

14. If I were a plant, I'd be a _____.

15. If I could change my name, I'd be _____.

16. The person I most like to talk to is _____.

17. I support _____.

18. The most influential person in my life has been _____
_____.

19. The most important thing to me is _____.

20. My greatest wish is _____.

Take time to ask yourself who or what may have influenced your responses. Were you able to put your feelings and thoughts into words? Did you discover anything new about yourself? Have you ever wondered why you think the way you do? What you think and how well you express your thoughts will determine your effectiveness as a communicator. You not only communicate ideas, you communicate yourself. The better you know yourself, the better you will be able to share that self with others.

CHAPTER TWO

Famous First Words
Visual Aids Speeches

Terms to Learn

stage fright	*problem-solution pattern*
audience analysis	*introduction*
purpose sentence	*body*
chronological pattern	*conclusion*
spatial pattern	*slogan*
topical pattern	*jingle*

Learning to speak publicly, to present ideas through the oral presentation, takes much time and effort. It involves both the matter and the manner of the speech. The matter, being the material presented, and the manner, the way in which it is presented, are equally important. Beginning speakers should realize that speech making is a part of our everyday lives. When you try to persuade your parents to let you do something which they are dead set against, you are speaking persuasively; and it is most likely that the speech is well planned and rehearsed. At some time, you may be asked to present a book report or introduce a guest speaker. Regardless of the type of speech or the size of the audience, the same rules apply when it comes to the mechanics of good speech making.

Preparation Overcomes Stage Fright

Being well prepared for speaking will help greatly in controlling your nervousness. This nervousness you feel when appearing as a speaker or performer before an audience is called **stage fright**. Convincing yourself that you are not going to fail can reduce your stage fright. Say these words to yourself, "I am prepared. I *will* do a good job on my speech. The audience will be interested in my speech topic." You can see how saying these positive things to yourself can put you in the right frame of mind for getting up in front of an audience. Too many speakers say, "My speech isn't going to be very good. I don't want to do this." Saying negative things like this will produce feelings of failure before you ever speak.

Gaining experience as a speaker will also reduce your fear of speaking. The more you get up in front of an audience, the more at ease you will become. Try to remember that most people get some form of stage fright. It may be seen as sweaty palms, a dry mouth or shaking knees. Another way of controlling this nervous tension is by focusing on your topic and your audience and not on yourself. Being well prepared and thinking positively are your best bets for overcoming stage fright.

Visual Aids

During those first speaking experiences, you sometimes wonder what to do with your hands. You are extremely self-conscious because you know all audience members' eyes are on you. One way to reduce the pressure of speech making is to provide something for the audience to look at. Several activities at the end of this chapter will provide the opportunity to do speeches with visual aids. This type of speech will make beginning speeches much easier. The audience will be focusing on the visual aid during the speech. This will mean audience eye contact will be divided between you and what you show. By the time you have spoken several times with visual aids, you realize that there's really no reason for your stage fright. At the same time your stage fright is reduced, your confidence is increased and you will have begun to take control as a speaker.

Planning your speech ahead of time is the first rule of good speaking. Speech preparation involves more than just getting up in front of a group of people to speak. You have to know what you are going to say. You have to prepare.

Audience Analysis

First, you select a topic that interests both you and your audience. Audience analysis is important because you need to know everything you can about the background, attitude and interests of those who will be listening to you. Selecting a purpose for speaking is what makes a speech different from an ordinary conversation. Speeches have direction, and you must know where you are headed with your words. Will you be speaking to interest, inform, stimulate, persuade or entertain? Remember that you will be the expert on your speech topic.

Choosing a topic with which you are already familiar will make speech preparation easier. The audience will also be able to tell if you are interested in your topic. Show both knowledge and enthusiasm regarding your speech topic, and you will generate audience interest.

Know the Intent of Your Speech

It is a good idea to decide upon the specific purpose of your speech; that is, precisely what you want the listeners to learn or do once they have heard the information. You must be very specific as you write a **purpose sentence,** a single sentence stating the intent of your speech. A sample purpose sentence might read: The purpose of this speech is to inform the audience about the proper care of a dog as a pet. Remember that the subject must fit the time allotted for your speech.

Some speeches require more than your personal knowledge of the subject. If your topic information seems shallow, you will want to add research to your speech. Support for your ideas may be material which comes from surveys, experts in the field, books, magazines and newspapers. Your researched information can be in the form of facts, statistics, illustrations, specific instances, narratives, examples, humor or quotations. You decide just exactly how much and what type of research information is needed to interest and inform your audience.

Every Speech Has Its Own Organizational Pattern

Many jobs are done simultaneously as the speech preparation process takes place. As you select your topic and begin preparation of the material, you will also decide on the organizational pattern to be used in your speech. There are several ways to put your materials together. The possible patterns include chronological, spatial, topical or problem-solution. You do not have to organize your speech using any of these techniques, but they will prove helpful as you gain experience as a speaker.

Chronological order develops in the same order that the events happen. A speech which discusses the history of women's rights could be put into this organizational pattern.

A *spatial* order uses space arrangements to tie the parts of a speech together. If your speech deals with a specific place, such as a vacation spot, this pattern would prove useful.

Another organizational pattern is *topical*, referring to the subject broken down into parts. All of the smaller parts fit together to form the whole topic. Speech topics for this pattern might be types of fishing or events at a gymnastic meet.

The fourth pattern, *problem-solution*, presents a problem that exists and develops a solution to the problem. A topic which could fit into this type of organizational pattern would be helping our senior citizens remain a vital and active part of our society.

Choosing an organizational pattern will depend upon the material you want to present about your topic, your style and creativity as a speaker, and the direction and purpose of the speech.

Having chosen a topic, researched it, and selected your organizational pattern, you will be ready to begin a speech outline. Write your outline in complete sentences. Forming your ideas into complete thoughts prior to your oral presentation is very helpful. Most people think that they can speak without advance outline preparation. These talented individuals are few, believe me. It takes time and hard work to prepare and present a good speech. The outline is essential if you are going to master the art of good speaking.

A speech is divided into three parts — an introduction, a body and a conclusion. The *introduction* should get the attention of the audience. It should tune the audience into the speaker and the topic, allowing them to concentrate on the material ahead. The *body* of the speech is the subject matter, your personal knowledge plus any researched material you add to your speech. The conclusion ties all materials of the speech together. It brings your speech to a close.

Several Ways to Begin a Speech

One of the biggest questions you will have as a speaker is, "How do I begin?" You can begin your speech a number of ways. You may want to begin your speech with a question. Ask your audience a rhetorical question which has to do with your topic. It will allow your audience to start thinking about your speech topic.

A story is another form of introduction. Open your speech by telling a story which connects with your subject. It may be a personal story or an anecdote which relates to the topic.

Get your audience's attention by using a "startler." Startle your audience by increasing your volume and/or using heightened energy to deliver a remark which directly links with your speech idea. Using a series of ideas, questions or words which pertains to your topic is another option for a speech introduction. A quotation may be an interesting way to tune in to the topic. A song, a poem or joke may be used to arouse the interest of the audience members as long as it relates to the subject.

Choose the type of introduction which best suits the style of speech you plan to present. Arrange your introduction ideas, body material and concluding remarks into an organized outline which will be helpful as you deliver your speech.

This skeleton of your ideas will begin with the purpose sentence. Keeping these important words in your mind will guide you as you develop your speech. Next, put the idea you have chosen for your introduction into a complete sentence. The body of your speech will contain two or three main heads (I, II, III). The main heads will support the purpose sentence. Under each main head will be subheads (A, B, C) which relate to the main heads. Any subdivisions (1, 2, 3) under the subheads provide support for subheads. As you gain experience in speech writing and speech making you can determine the type of outlining which is best for you.

```
     I. (Main Head)
        A. (Subhead)
        B. (Subhead)
        C. (Subhead)
           1. (Subdivision)
           2. (Subdivision)
           3. (Subdivision)
    II. (Main Head)
        A. (Subhead)
        B. (Subhead)
        C. (Subhead)
           1. (Subdivision)
           2. (Subdivision)
           3. (Subdivision)
```

Writing your speech ideas in complete thoughts allows you to think about what you want to say and how you plan to say it. It plants the exact wording in your brain so that perhaps you can recall those words when you speak.

Requirements of a Strong Conclusion

The only thing left in the speech writing process is the conclusion. Just because you have completed giving information does not mean you have finished with your speech. You must briefly emphasize the main points of your speech. The closing should provide a brief summary which brings the main points of the speech into final focus. No new material should be introduced in the conclusion as it only confuses the audience. It should be evident to your listeners that you are "wrapping things up."

The conclusion should be left to restate what you have previously stated in the other parts of your speech. Remember, as the introduction allows for a speaker to give a positive first impression, so does a conclusion provide the opportunity to leave a good, lasting impression with the audience. Do not omit any part of a speech because each part has a vital function of equal importance.

Before you deliver your speech orally, you will want to expand the outline into the exact words you wish to present. The full manuscript should never be memorized. The possibility of forgetting important parts of your speech is too great when you try to use word-for-word memorization. A better method would be to write the speech in paragraph form as you would like to present it. Familiarize yourself with your exact wording by going over your speech several times.

Transfer the main ideas of your speech to index cards for use in the oral presentation of your speech. Remember, never write complete sentences on your note cards, but just brief notes to give you assistance during your speech, if needed. It is advisable to memorize your introduction and conclusion so that both beginning and ending of your speech are strong. Refer to your note cards during the body of your speech, never read from them.

Methods of Rehearsing a Speech

Rehearsing your speech is the final step in speech preparation. Try recording your speech on a tape recorder and playing it back to hear how you sound. Another practice method involves delivering the speech while facing a mirror so that you may see how you look. You may get an actual critique ahead of delivery time if you can secure an audience with which to practice. All of these rehearsal techniques provide essential feedback so that you will make the necessary improvements to produce an excellent speech.

There are several visual aid speech ideas provided here which will allow you to practice the speech writing techniques discussed in this chapter.

Object Speech

The first visual aid speech is called the object speech. As previously discussed, beginning speakers have difficulty in their first speeches knowing what to do with their hands and where to look. Having an object to hold is like having a security blanket. It gives you something with which to refer, something to look at besides your audience, and something to do with your hands. With the audience's eye contact divided between you and your object, you will find that you are a little more at ease. The object speech gives you experience in front of an audience and practice organizing your ideas without much difficulty. It is a fun, easy speech designed to give you an enjoyable first speaking experience.

ACTIVITY — Object Speech

OBJECTIVE

1. To promote self-confidence in speech making by using an object as a visual aid.

INSTRUCTIONS

1. Bring an object to class.

2. The object will need to be a practical object.

3. Show the object and completely describe it.

4. Tell the uses of the object. These may be practical or humorous or both.

5. Tell anything else that pertains to the object that may be of interest to the audience.

6. The speech may be either informative or entertaining.

7. Time limit for the speech is one to two minutes.

Topic Suggestions

1. tennis racket
2. pen
3. gum
4. belt
5. rubber band
6. toothbrush
7. pillowcase
8. newspaper
9. toilet paper
10. pan
11. telephone
12. piece of paper
13. coke bottle
14. Band-Aid
15. rope

Chalk Talk

The next speech idea is called the chalk talk. This activity is a good speech to use following the object speech. Again, visual aids are used to help reduce stage fright. The student will use the chalkboard to illustrate in any way possible the material presented in the speech. The speaker must concentrate on what is being said, not simply what is put on the board. This type of speech gives the speaker something to do during the speech and provides the audience with something to look at besides the speaker, thereby relieving the pressure felt by the speaker. A student can be as creative as he would like to be with a speech of this nature.

ACTIVITY — Chalk Talk

O B J E C T I V E

1. To promote self-confidence in speech making by using the chalkboard as a helpful visual aid.

I N S T R U C T I O N S

1. Choose a subject which will lend itself to illustration.
2. Prepare a speech outline and drawings to accompany the speech.
3. The drawings should help the audience understand the speech subject more clearly.
4. Talk about a particular subject *while* using the chalkboard. Talk and draw, draw and talk.
5. This speech is not a test of artistic ability. Simple drawings are best for this assignment.
6. The speech may be either entertaining or informative.
7. Time limit for the speech is two or three minutes.
8. The board work may be words, drawings, diagrams, symbols, any-

---

> thing at all which enhances the speech topic. Allow the speech to come to life through the board work.
>
> 9. Use as much of the board as possible, working from left to right.
> 10. Be aware of the audience, and be sure not to block board work.

Topic Suggestions

1. road signs
2. hair styles
3. facial expressions
4. football plays
5. how to make a banana split
6. holidays
7. birthday party decorations

8. seasons
9. sports
10. how to decorate a Christmas tree
11. the perfect vacation
12. a day at the amusement park
13. choosing a pet

The Demonstration Speech

Incorporating necessary movement into speech making helps to increase interest. Watching someone demonstrate a process as he/she tells you about it also increases learning potential. We are a visually oriented society. Learning by seeing is one important way we communicate messages. The demonstration speech is commonly referred to as the "how to" speech. You will show the audience how to do something. Your speech topic could be a variety of subjects, but choosing a topic with which you are familiar is of utmost importance. Being familiar with the process you are demonstrating, you will feel more comfortable in front of an audience.

ACTIVITY — The Demonstration Speech

OBJECTIVE

1. To promote self-confidence in speech making by using objects with which to demonstrate a process.

INSTRUCTIONS

1. Demonstrate a process to the audience.
2. Tell what you are going to demonstrate, including the end results.
3. List all essentials, ingredients or equipment needed.

4. Demonstrate the entire process, step by step.

5. Emphasize points of interest and concern, such as common errors or helpful hints.

6. Show the results.

7. Review the materials and procedure to reinforce the process.

8. Remember to *show* the process, don't just tell about it.

9. Be sure to maintain good eye contact throughout the speech.

10. Time limit for the speech is four to five minutes.

Topic Suggestions

1. how to wrap a birthday present
2. how to play golf
3. how to organize a folder
4. how to make a banana split
5. how to brush your teeth
6. how to apply make-up
7. how to use a camera
8. how to splint an injury
9. how to care for a dog
10. how to diaper a baby
11. how to throw and catch a football
12. how to snow ski
13. how to braid hair
14. how to pop popcorn
15. how to paint with watercolors
16. how to spot someone cheating on a test
17. how to play an instrument
18. how to save someone from choking
19. how to make a salad
20. how to make cookies

The Commercial

What could be more fun than creating and writing your own commercial? An interesting and educational way to introduce the commercial speech is to list your favorite commercials. This can be done individually, in small groups or by having the entire group brainstorm by putting ideas on the chalkboard. Discuss what characteristics commercials possess. What makes them likeable? What makes them memorable? Many commercials use a catchy word or phrase which makes the product more memorable. This clever word or phrase is called a **slogan**. If the product uses a catchy phrase or verse which is sung or put to music, then it is referred to as a **jingle**. Both slogans and jingles are very effective marketing strategies. The consumer, or person using the product, has a way to identify the product and hopefully will buy it. Oftentimes, a jingle is so catchy that a person continues to hum or sing the tune long after hearing the commercial. Make a list of current slogans and jingles. Have each person stand and deliver his phrase and allow the audience to respond using choral response as they call out the name of the product. Preparing flash cards with slogans and jingles ahead of class time is another fun way to use choral response.

ACTIVITY — The Commercial

O B J E C T I V E S

1. To promote self-confidence in speech making by using a product as a visual aid in delivering a commercial.
2. To develop persuasive speaking skills.

I N S T R U C T I O N S

1. Write an original commercial.
2. The minimum length of the commercial will be 100 words. No maximum length.
3. The speech will be completely memorized.
4. You may adapt ideas from radio and television.
5. Repeat the name of the product several times, remembering the name should also be original.
6. Use a jingle or slogan or both.
7. Make and bring the product for use in the speech.
8. Music may be incorporated into the commercial.
9. No off-color or offensive words or ideas may be used.
10. You may use any other type of visual aid to help sell the product.
11. Use vocal energy, appropriate movement and good eye contact to sell the product.
12. Optional — videotape all commercials.

Videotaping the commercials provides the opportunity for personal critiques. Each speaker may watch the videotape of his/her performance and make oral or written comments.

Topic Suggestions

1. soft drink
2. shampoo
3. toothpaste
4. bubblegum
5. soap
6. hair spray
7. cereal
8. cologne or perfume
9. deodorant
10. toilet paper
11. diapers
12. fast food restaurants
13. dog food
14. paper towels
15. pain reliever
16. breath mint
17. mouthwash
18. bug spray
19. laundry detergent
20. candy bar

School Commercial

Commercials don't necessarily have to sell products, they can promote other things. Your next assignment will be a group project in which you promote your school. Don't hold back, have fun with this one! This speech is one which can be shared with other classes. Perform your polished commercials at an open house, PTA meeting or a pep rally. Your audience will love them!

ACTIVITY — School Commercial

O B J E C T I V E S

1. To promote participation in a group project.
2. To promote school pride.

I N S T R U C T I O N S

1. Get into small groups (three to six people).

2. Write a commercial promoting your school.

3. The speech should emphasize the many positive assets the school possesses.

4. Use a slogan and jingle in your school commercial.

5. The minimum length of the speech will be 150 words. No maximum.

6. Each participant will have an equal part in the commercial.

7. The commercial may be informative or entertaining.

8. Use some type of visual aid in the presentation to communicate your ideas.

9. Music and costumes may be incorporated.

CHAPTER THREE

Two's Company
Partner Speeches

Terms to Learn

open-mindedness
role playing
introduction (presenter's) speech
acceptance speech

rap
cue
timing

"Two's company" is a comforting thought for beginning speakers. Knowing you will not be performing solo in front of an audience can greatly reduce stage fright. The cliché "two heads are better than one" can easily apply to the partner speech-making process. Creative power can be doubled with both speakers contributing ideas. Some speakers feel they have a greater chance of success when working with a partner. Many beginning speakers don't trust their own talents or abilities. They are not sure they can do it alone. The fear of speaking, as with many other kinds of fear, does not seem as threatening with another person close by. Partner speeches not only help build self-confidence as they decrease anxiety, but they also encourage further development of interpersonal skills. While working with another person, you learn to contribute and compromise. You learn to share, to open up and to listen. If problems arise as you make decisions on the direction of your speech, you learn to work through them. You strengthen your problem-solving skills during the speech planning process.

Open-Mindedness

The ability to listen to all sides of the question or situation before making a decision or drawing a conclusion is to be encouraged in partner speech work. If your partner seems forceful and opinionated, try to use tact and diplomacy as you make helpful suggestions. Generally, the more cooperative you are in the preparation, the better the outcome.

Don't think that because you have someone with which to work that the speech will be easy. On the contrary, it will be harder. Learning to work slowly through a speech with another person requires patience. You must learn to accept their ideas while, at the same time, dismissing ideas of your own. The building process may not always be easy, but sharing in the success of the project with a friend or classmate is well worth the extra effort.

An interview, a common procedure for gaining information, can be a very interesting and entertaining partner speech. Interviews are conducted by a variety of people in diversified situations. Sportscasters conduct interviews with athletes. An employer questions a potential employee, and a talk-show host or hostess shows great skill as he/she interviews a celebrity.

There are several dos and don'ts in successful interviewing. Do prepare in advance by formulating appropriate questions. Show thorough knowledge of the interview topic. Don't ask questions which require a simple yes or no answer. Instead, ask clear thought-provoking questions which provide information of interest to your audience. Do let your interviewee have ample time to think about and answer the questions. Be aware of your partner's verbal and nonverbal cues and act accordingly. Read between the lines. Ask yourself, "Have we exhausted this particular subject or is the interviewee interested in pursuing the questioning in this area?" Listen attentively to what is being said; don't monopolize the conversation. Try to keep the interview moving and on the subject. Don't jump from topic to topic, use smooth transitions as you move from one subject to the next.

To allow for the interview to move smoothly, you must organize your ideas. Your introduction should introduce your situation and speakers, depending on the specific situation. State the purpose of the interview and lead in with an easy question. Next, organize your questions in the body of your speech. Be flexible. If your interviewee's responses change the initial direction of the speech, follow up with related questions. Go back to your prepared outline when you can without letting your speech become choppy and hard to follow. Wrap up your speech with your final questions and then conclude by summarizing the responses from the interview.

The Interview (Role Playing)

The interview, in itself, incorporates many beneficial communication skills. A way of making this standard speech new and exciting is to allow for fun creativeness through role playing, a way of acting out a situation to understand it better. You have the opportunity to portray a person other than yourself. You take on all characteristics of that person, including vocal qualities, facial expressions and physical gestures. Costuming and props will also be fun additions to the selected setting you choose for the interview. You can keep it very simple, using only minimal items to suggest the idea or you may "go all out" as you execute the interview. Be creative and original as you choose your interview format and who your interviewer and interviewee will be.

ACTIVITY — The Interview (Role Playing)

O B J E C T I V E S

1. To develop interviewing skills.
2. To provide a prepared role playing experience.
3. To develop interpersonal communication skills.

INSTRUCTIONS

1. Decide the identity of the interviewer and interviewee.
2. Decide on an appropriate interview format.
3. Devise a list of questions and answers to be used as an interview script.
4. Choose an idea which works well for both participants.
5. The interview should be shared equally with lines and responsibilities.
6. Be creative. Let your interview seem spontaneous and unrehearsed.
7. Organize ideas with an introduction, body and conclusion.
8. Demonstrate knowledge of the topic and/or guest.
9. Maintain a polite and interested attitude.
10. Time limit for the speech is 4-5 minutes.
11. You may incorporate appropriate music to create atmosphere.
12. Rehearse your speech. Practice several times to familiarize yourself with the questions and answers.

Topic Suggestions

1. psychiatrist and patient
2. sportscaster and athlete
3. host and celebrity
4. on-the-scene reporter and eyewitness
5. employer and potential employee
6. lawyer and witness
7. police detective and suspect
8. politician and reporter
9. reporter and performer
10. any fictional character and talk-show host

Presenter's Introduction and Acceptance Speech

Introduction of a Speaker

In order to present an award or gift to someone worthy of being honored, you must first know how to introduce the recipient. The **introduction** or **presenter's speech** is one in which a person introduces a speaker to an audience. There are various reasons for the introduction. The person could be a guest speaker or an honoree worthy of recognition. Learning how to adequately prepare the audience for the speaker is essential if you are to avoid boring the audience and embarrassing the speaker and yourself. To adequately honor someone and recognize his/her achievements, you must familiarize yourself with the speaker's talents and credits. You must inform the audience of the special qualities of the speaker as you establish his/her credibility. In preparing this type of speech, consider not only the speaker, but also the audience and the reason for the presentation. Try to offer enough information without going overboard. Keep the introduction brief. The speech may include the speaker's name, background, special qualifications, honors, or any other noteworthy achievements. Try to be factual and accurate when describing the speaker's notables. Avoid flowery praise. The last thing you want to do is embarrass the speaker. Say enough to make the speaker feel proud and worthy of your remarks.

If an award or gift is given, try not to emphasize it. You are honoring the person and the deed, not the award. Avoid drawing attention to yourself. Your goal is to focus on the person receiving the award. Above all, convey sincerity.

The Acceptance Speech

The natural counterpart of the introduction or presenter's speech is the acceptance speech. The **acceptance speech** is one in which the speaker accepting the honor conveys appreciation for the recognition given. This speech has the specific purpose of thanking those giving the award and those responsible for helping the recipient achieve the goals necessary to attain such an accomplishment. As with the introduction, the acceptance speech should be brief and to the point. When delivering this type of speech, you should express your gratitude modestly and sincerely. Recognize those people who were involved or responsible for helping you achieve your success. Don't forget to show appreciation for the gift given. You may want to inform the audience about any future plans related to the award. Try to leave your audience with the feeling that you are truly grateful and genuinely deserving of the gift or award.

The presenter's introduction and acceptance speeches are excellent partner speeches. Both presenter and receiver have specific things to say and do in their respective speeches, but can work together combining ideas.

Role playing can also be used with the introduction and acceptance speeches as you choose an interesting and original idea for the presenter and receiver. Create an actual award to be given to the recipient at some time during the presentation. It could be anything that pertains to or represents the award — a check, a trophy, or a plaque.

This speech can be formal with a serious tone, or it can be humorous and entertaining. The ideas for the introduction and acceptance speech are limitless if you will use your imagination!

ACTIVITY — Presenter's Introduction/Acceptance Speech

O B J E C T I V E S

1. To gain experience in writing and delivering a presenter's introduction.
2. To gain experience in writing and delivering an acceptance speech.
3. To develop interpersonal communication skills.

I N S T R U C T I O N S

1. Decide upon type of award, presenter and recipient.
2. Write two speeches as you work in pairs.
3. One speech will present an award.
4. One speech will receive an award.
5. The speech which presents the award should:
   a. make appropriate remarks to the audience.
   b. give reasons for the award.
   c. tell something about the receiver of the award.
   d. introduce the award winner.
6. The speech which accepts the award should:

---

a. address the audience.

b. express gratitude for the gift.

c. give thanks and credit where deserved.

d. give remarks for future plans or help.

e. repeat thank-yous.

7. The speech may be informative or entertaining.

8. Time limit for each speech should be at least one minute in length.

9. Optional, but advisable. Make the award to use in your presentation. Make sure it pertains to the area of recognition.

Topic Suggestions

1. athletic award (swimming, football, golf, etc.)
2. scholarship (cash awards in certain subjects)
3. academic award (top speech student, etc.)
4. academy award
5. music award
6. record holder
7. community service (fireman, policeman, etc.)
8. new invention
9. scientific discovery
10. outstanding performance
11. championship
12. cash prize
13. beauty contest winner
14. dance contest winner
15. crazy off-the-wall award
16. volunteer
17. job performance

Presenter - me

A Rap Speech

Making a speech in front of a group is not the only way to communicate an idea which is important to you. There are other interesting ways to convey meaningful messages. For instance, if you are presenting a message to young people, you might want a **rap** to get the message to the group. An old idea can be given new life with a novel style of presentation. Using the upbeat rhythm and rhyme of rap, you can deliver a message in a creative and entertaining way. Writing a rap is similar to writing poetry. You use easy flowing verses which have a definite beat and generally use end rhyme.

Lines may be delivered solo or in unison. Lines can be broken up where half of a line is done in duet and the other half by one single speaker. A line may have a word which requires emphasis so the speaker delivers the line, and the second speaker joins in to accentuate the particular word. Using a variety of delivery styles will make your rap more effective.

There are several tips for effective delivery of the rap speech. Try to keep the rhythm consistent. It is important that both participants stay synchronized. Being together means that timing is accurate and cues are picked up appropriately. A *cue* simply means any word, movement, sound or action that signals you to perform the next word or action. *Timing* is of utmost importance as you use pause and pace to achieve the effect you desire. You emphasize a line or a movement so that it builds and becomes more climactic than the one preceding it.

When delivering the rap, you should use well planned movement to create interest. The movement should be motivated, it should have meaning, be animated, and bring the rap to life with descriptive gestures, facial expressions and collaborative actions. The action needn't be elaborate, it should merely enhance the message presented.

Try for crisp, clear pronunciation of your words with good articulation. Even though you incorporate movement, the words are still the most important part of the rap speech.

Share your talents and hard work with others by organizing the raps into a program with a central theme. Present the program to a group who would benefit from the message in the raps or just simply enjoy the entertainment.

ACTIVITY — A Rap Speech

O B J E C T I V E S

1. To prepare and deliver a rap which uses rhythm, rhyme, emphasis and movement within the speech.
2. To develop interpersonal communication skills.

I N S T R U C T I O N S

1. Create a two- to three-minute rap on a worthwhile topic.
2. The assignment must have equal parts.
3. Break up the lines using a variety of emphasis.
4. Use both rhythm and rhyme in writing the speech.
5. Memorize the assignment. Use of note cards would only hinder the performance.
6. Use gestures, facial expressions and movement.
7. If rhythm percussion sounds are used, they must be man-made, not electronic.

Topic Suggestions

1. just say "no" to drugs
2. buckle up for safety
3. cleaner environment
4. school spirit
5. any major news event
6. physical fitness
7. stay in school versus dropping out
8. any topic within a course of study

The Telephone Conversation

Conversation is an everyday part of interpersonal communication. It is when two or more people share ideas through informal talk. Telephone conversations share the same rules as face-to-face conversations. As a good conversationalist, you should show an interest in people, broaden your range of topics, develop language skills, avoid being dogmatic and, especially, keep away from gossip.

There are many general rules for correct telephone usage. First, when calling someone, allow six rings and do not hang up during a ring. Be considerate of the time of day. Social calls should be made at a time when they are least likely to be a disturbance. Always identify yourself as soon as someone answers. Give your full name and then ask to speak to the person you are calling. An example would be, "Hello, this is Joe Lincoln. May I speak to Mary, please?" When the requested person answers, introduce yourself again. Speak clearly into the receiver, holding it about one-half inch from your mouth. Get to the purpose of the call, tell the other person as briefly as possible why you are calling. Avoid tying up the line for long periods of time and don't monopolize the conversation. The caller is responsible for bringing the conversation to a close. If a message must be left, the caller should leave clear, precise information. The person taking the message should record the exact time of call, the number to reach the caller and the exact message. Repeating the message back to the caller can prevent any misinformation. Whether you are calling or answering, courtesy and friendliness are the most important characteristics of telephone use.

Mock telephone conversations are a great activity with which to conclude the partner speech unit. By preparing two speeches, you quickly learn the right and wrong way to conduct yourself on the telephone.

One speech includes as many no-nos as the speakers can possibly include; all telephone rules are broken. The second speech is a perfect example of telephone etiquette. What an interesting way to learn the very important rules of good telephone use!

ACTIVITY — The Telephone Conversation

O B J E C T I V E S

1. To develop good telephone etiquette.
2. To develop interpersonal communication skills as students work together on partner speeches.

I N S T R U C T I O N S

1. In pairs, write two mock telephone conversations.
2. One speech will be a comedy of intended errors — break all the rules.
3. The second speech will follow good telephone conversation form.
4. Deliver both speeches orally.
5. Discuss the strong and weak points of each conversation after the set of phone calls has been presented.

This speech can be such fun using phones as props — one for each speaker. Using this type of activity, the rules can be quickly learned without resorting to boring memorization techniques. The speakers are involved in a creative process which allows them to have fun as they learn.

CHAPTER FOUR

Special Delivery

"Methods of Delivery" Speeches

Terms to Learn

delivery
volume
inflection
pitch
rate
verbalized pause
vocal quality
clarity

articulation
pronunciation
gestures
impromptu delivery
extemporaneous delivery
memorized delivery
manuscript delivery

People are involved in making decisions every day of their lives. These choices range in importance from what to wear to work, to whom will get your vote for President of the United States. Learning to trust your judgment on the choices you must make becomes easier as you mature. You learn to interpret and understand why you act and react a certain way in a situation. The decisions you make are based upon your own personal background, experiences and feelings.

The events which have taken place in your life are totally unique to you. No other person on this earth has seen what you have seen, heard what you have heard, been where you have been, or felt what you

41

have felt. When you communicate with others, you share a part of yourself. Your audience gets a closer look at the real you.

This chapter provides you several opportunities to make decisions and give your reasons for making such choices. It also discusses the four main methods of speech delivery and the many ways to make your personal delivery as effective as possible.

The Audience Must Believe in You

To be effective, the audience must believe in you. As an effective communicator, you must be sincere. You hope that the audience will be receptive to your ideas. Share with your audience your knowledge on a particular subject. Your audience will want to listen because they feel what you have to say is worthwhile.

The speakers throughout history who were skilled communicators spoke with power and persuasiveness. To convince the audience that what you have to say is important and meaningful, you must speak with confidence and knowledge about your subject.

Show that both you and your speech have a direction. Organization is essential from beginning to end. Having a definite purpose is your guiding force in expressive speech writing.

The speaker's words are important and should be chosen carefully with the particular audience in mind so that the message is received and understood. Communicators should keep in mind the effect their nonverbal communication has on the audience. Facial expressions, physical appearance, body movement, eye contact and posture can all be used to further communicate the verbal message.

For the most part, a speaker will want to achieve a certain goal by the end of his presentation. You will want to have informed, persuaded, or entertained your audience members. If you are to be an effective speech communicator, you must refine the important speaking skills through practice in order to achieve the results you desire.

This chapter deals specifically with delivery. **Delivery** is the way to use your voice and body to present a speech to an audience. With every speech, you will choose a certain style or method of delivery. A speech also deals with the speaker's personal delivery. This involves nonverbal messages such as appearance, facial expressions, voice, eye contact, gestures and body movement during the speech.

Communication Involves Much More Than Speaking

You are communicating before you ever open your mouth and say a word. Your appearance transmits a message to your audience about you and your attitude. The audience can tell if you are nervous or confident, prepared or unprepared, interested in speaking or uninterested. Look as if you are enthusiastic and well prepared as you give your first impression to your audience.

Your voice says so much about you. It also affects whether your audience will "tune in" or "tune out" to your speech. Volume, rate, pitch, vocal quality and clarity should be used together to produce effective and appropriate speech. Vary the **volume** — the loudness or softness of sound. Above all, be sure all members of the audience can hear you. Allow for natural inflection or change in the pitch level of your voice. **Pitch** is the placement of your voice on the musical scale — or more simply, the highness or lowness of a sound. The pitch should change naturally and help support the meaning of the spoken words. Use a variety of **rates**, or speed at which you speak. Slowing down to emphasize an important point allows listeners to comprehend. Avoid using **verbalized** and **vocalized pauses**, such as "well," "er," "ah," "um," or "you know," which are very distracting. **Vocal quality**, which refers to the sound of your voice, should be considered, although it is difficult to change. A nasal quality or raspy voice can be distracting, so be aware of how your voice sounds to others. **Clarity**, the clearness of the speaker's words, is vital. Articulation and correct pronunciation are essential skills to be encouraged if the audience is to fully understand the speech message. **Articulation** is the process of forming sounds into words, the way you use your teeth, tongue, lips, lower jaw, and soft palate to produce clear, crisp speech. **Pronunciation** is the production of correct sounds and syllable stresses when speaking. An example of poor articulation would be to say "wacha doin'?" for the question, "What are you doing?" An example of poor pro-nunciation would be the word "warsh" for the correct "wash." Be careful not to be lazy with your speech. Try not to let regional dialect be too noticeable. Strive to have good standard speech, that which is accepted by the prominent speakers of the day and that which is considered correct usage by the dictionary.

Nonverbal Communication

Nonverbal language, including facial expressions, gestures, movement, and eye contact should be natural and motivated by the words of your speech. Eye contact should be extended, not merely quick glances. Look at the audience for several seconds and be sure to include all audience members. Eye contact will give you an idea of how the audience is responding to your speech. This is how you check for understanding. Your **gestures**, the movements of your head, arms and upper body, are used to emphasize an idea or main point. The gestures must be big enough to be seen in order to be understood. A small  amount of movement during a speech is acceptable. It should not take the form of pacing, over-gesturing, weight-shifting or nervous fidgeting. It should help make the message clearer and more meaningful.

There are several different methods of speech delivery. Public speakers choose from one of four basic methods, depending on the situation. There are many advantages and disadvantages to each style of presentation.

The Impromptu Method

If you were to speak at a meeting without use of notes and with very little preparation, you would be using the impromptu method of delivery. You organize your ideas and choose your words as you speak. The key thing to remember is to keep your speech simple, formulate one central idea and concentrate on developing it. One great advantage to impromptu speaking is the fact that it sounds natural and spontaneous. Becoming a proficient impromptu speaker is very beneficial because of its everyday usefulness. If you are ever asked to speak on the spur of the moment without prior notice, you will feel more comfortable thinking on your feet and be able to better express yourself. Its major disadvantage is, of course, lack of time to prepare, therefore, causing it to sound unprepared. Inexperienced impromptu speakers tend to ramble without ever saying anything. Practice is the way to master the impromptu method of speaking.

Here's an activity where you can try the impromptu method of delivery. Another activity which explores impromptu speaking is offered in Chapter Eight.

ACTIVITY — The Impromptu Method

O B J E C T I V E S

1. To gain experience using the impromptu speech delivery.
2. To develop the ability to make choices through reasoning.

I N S T R U C T I O N S

1. You must give up life's modern conveniences.
2. The conveniences are:
   a. telephone
   b. radio, stereo, television
   c. refrigerator
   d. automobile
   e. bathroom
   f. washing machine and dryer
3. What will you give up first, second, third, etc.?
4. Give reasons for your choices.
5. Organize your speech with an introduction, body and conclusion.
6. Present the speech using the impromptu style of delivery.

Be sure to try the impromptu speech idea in Chapter Eight if this impromptu speech idea is too difficult.

The Extemporaneous Speech

The next method of delivery we will explore is the extemporaneous style. Extemporaneous speaking means speaking from an outline of ideas without memorizing an exact pattern of words. This type of presentation is most common and generally, most effective. The speaker usually puts the outline on note cards, using only key words or phrases. It is helpful to write out the opening and closing and any information that needs to be stated exactly. Practicing aloud to rehearse key phrases will help you to present ideas which flow smoothly. One advantage to this type of speech is its ability to allow you to respond and adapt to audience feedback. When you are speaking from an outline, you have more freedom to adjust the speech to meet the needs of the speaking situation. By using note cards, you have the chance to be more personal with your audience. You can move about and gesture more freely because you aren't limited by a manuscript or full-length speech. Your style will be more conversational as you fill in the outline as you speak. To present the best extemporaneous speech possible, practice on your feet with an imaginary or real audience. Work from your prepared outline.

A major disadvantage to this style of delivery is that it gives the speaker a sense of false confidence. You feel you have completed the speech when the outline is complete. The most important step, that of practice, is somehow forgotten. The end result is that during the delivery, the speaker realizes something vital is missing from the speech. This unpleasant experience needn't happen if you can strike a balance between the desired spontaneity and the required practice of this type of speech delivery style.

Practice using the extemporaneous style of delivery with the following speech activity.

ACTIVITY — The Extemporaneous Speech

OBJECTIVES

1. To gain experience using the extemporaneous method of speech delivery.
2. To develop the ability to make choices through reasoning.

1. Make a two-minute speech on the six professionals listed below. Rank them in order of their importance in respect to the ones which have contributed the most to our society.
   a. preacher
   b. farmer
   c. scientist
   d. artisan (actor, painter, architect, writer)
   e. politician
   f. teacher
2. Have reasons for the placement of each professional.
3. Prepare a good introduction which in some way relates to your order of choices.
4. Conclude with an effective summary of your ideas.
5. Present the speech using the extemporaneous style of delivery.

The Memorized Speech

The third method for delivering speeches is memorization. This method calls for word-for-word memorized delivery. Few occasions call for totally memorized speeches in which the speaker writes out the entire speech, memorizes it and delivers it without note cards or a manuscript. The main advantage to memorized delivery is that it leaves the speaker free to move about and have direct eye contact with the audience without having to worry about handling cards or papers. The greatest disadvantage to this style of delivery is the possibility of forgetting the speech. The mind goes blank, and silence falls over the entire audience. Your memory has failed you, and there is no way out. Another downfall to the memorized method is the fact that the audience feedback has little to do with the direction of the speech. No matter how the audience reacts, the memorized version will be the same; and therefore, lacks spontaneity. As with each style of delivery, this particular method does have a time and place when it can be beneficial and used to produce the desired result.

Incorporate what you have learned in this chapter and present the following speech using the memorized style of delivery.

ACTIVITY — The Memorized Speech

O B J E C T I V E S

1. To gain experience using the memorized method of speech delivery.
2. To develop the ability to make choices through reasoning.

I N S T R U C T I O N S

1. Write a two-minute speech about six factors of life.
2. The factors are (1) friends, (2) education, (3) family, (4) money, (5) religion and (6) health.
3. Rank the factors in order of importance.
4. Give your personal reasons for the ranking.
5. Use a good introduction and conclusion relating to your choices.
6. Present the speech using the memorized method of delivery.

The Manuscript Speech

The fourth method of delivery which calls for you to write out the speech and read it aloud to the audience is called the manuscript method. This type of speech works well when you have very detailed information that you must state exactly. The main advantage to this style of speaking is that the speech can be delivered without the possibility of errors in important information. Misphrasing or lapses of memory do not pose a problem with manuscript readings. The disadvantages are lack of eye contact and minimal interaction with the audience. Any time a written speech is used, the speaker tends to be more confined. Gestures, movement and audience eye contact are limited by the manuscript in hand.

48

The deserted island speech is a story which demands the use of many details. This speech activity works well for the manuscript method of delivery.

ACTIVITY — The Manuscript Speech

O B J E C T I V E S

1. To gain experience in using the manuscript method of speech delivery.
2. To develop the ability to make choices through reasoning.

I N S T R U C T I O N S

1. Write a speech about the following situation. Trapped on a lonely deserted island are ten people. They are: a famous movie star, a noted scientist, a preacher or priest, a twelve-year-old boy, the Governor, the president of General Motors, a wealthy society couple, your best friend, and your mother.

2. In a helicopter, you happen upon the island where the ten people are stranded. Explain why you have a helicopter and why you land on the island.

3. What explanation do the people give as to the reason they are stranded? What has happened during your short stay on the island?

4. Give the identity of the ten people.

5. You have the ability to save only five people. The rest will be left to face an unknown fate.

6. Decide who you are going to save and why.

7. Write a complete story concerning every detail of your experience.

8. Try to include character dialog in your story.

9. The story may be serious or humorous.

10. Present the speech using the manuscript method of delivery.

Many speakers find that they can be most effective by combining speech delivery methods. For instance, try combining the extemporaneous method with the memorized style. By memorizing the introduction, conclusion and key sentences throughout the body of the speech and then delivering the remainder of the speech extemporaneously, the speaker has found a way to gain the advantages of each style.

Whatever method you choose to use in a given situation, remember that there are many ways in which you can enhance your delivery. By using variety in your voice and expressive body language, the verbal and nonverbal cues will come together to effectively communicate the intended message to your audience.

CHAPTER FIVE

Once Upon a Time
Storytelling

Terms to Learn

character
dialog
plot
conflict
climax
animation

point of view
narration
colorful language
connectives
setting
mood

Everyone has at some time or other been a storyteller. You recite your tale to an audience, hoping to get the reaction you desire. You might hope to elicit laughter, empathy or fear. Your story could be a personal experience, a strange incident or a most embarrassing moment. Children's fairy tales and folk tales certainly need a special touch when being told aloud. A speaker can benefit in so many ways by learning the skills necesssary to become a quality storyteller.

As you begin to tell an anecdote or relate a personal experience, you should consider the incidents of the story and the order in which they occur. A story must have details and description to bring it to life and make the story clearer to the audience. You will want the story to be vivid so that the audience members will be excited and stimulated. Vocal flexibility will work to set the appropriate mood and suggest characters in the story. A rich vocabulary will allow you to arouse their imaginations. The words the storyteller chooses will greatly affect the audience response.

Develop a Story Plan

Careful planning and practice will be essential to the success of your story. Consider who is involved in the story you are telling, when the story takes place, where the action occurs and what exactly happens. It's good to determine the high point of the story so that you can build to that point. Facial expressions and gestures will help to emphasize exciting or important parts of the story. No matter what kind of speech you might deliver, the techniques used by a storyteller will be very useful and will enhance any speaking project.

Fundamental to any story are the people in the story, the **characters.** The description and dialog should allow the listener to visualize what each character looks and feels like. The **dialog**, or words spoken by the characters, should reveal the emotions of the characters. The dialog brings the listeners closer to the characters allowing them to get to know the characters personally.

A well-told story has an interesting outline of action. The events which happen in a story are called the **plot**. The story should begin with a short, interesting opening. This will assure the audience's attention. Next, develop the events in a logical sequence. A **conflict**, some kind of a problem or a clash, is followed by a **climax**, the highest point of action in the story. The climax is also referred to as the turning point in the story as the events in the story all come together. The conclusion, or ending, brings all loose ends together as the story conflict is resolved.

Develop a Storytelling Style

Much of a good story involves description of the characters, the scene and the plot. Choice of language and details can be used to offer insight into the situation. Life can be breathed into the story through animation. **Animation** means that gestures, facial expressions, body language and vocal variety are used to enliven the presentation. Try to produce a unique manner of vocal delivery and body movements. Developing your own style takes much practice and experimentation, but it will be well worth the time and effort when you can thoroughly captivate an audience with your storytelling skills and techniques.

Most stories are told from first person *point of view*. This means the story is told as if the storyteller were an eyewitness to the action. Other points of view or perspectives from which a story can be told are second and third person. With second person point of view, the audience is spoken to by having the storyteller use the word "you." Third person point of view allows for the storyteller to observe what is taking place.

While learning storytelling techniques, you will also be exercising your imagination. You must suggest situations to which the audience can relate. They will put themselves in the situation you describe, if you do so imaginatively. Your listeners can experience the entire event vicariously.

Consider the Structure of Your Story

Stories consist mainly of narration and dialog. **Narration** is telling the events which happen in a story, and dialog consists of the words the characters speak. The stories can be fiction, nonfiction or personal experience. Fiction stories are stories which are not true; they are a creation of the imagination. Nonfiction involves true stories, such as biographies. Personal experience entails any story that is taken directly from the storyteller's own experiences in life.

Language is the device a storyteller uses to entice the listeners — to keep them listening. **Colorful language** conveys sights, sounds, smells, touch and tastes. The descriptions the storyteller uses should appeal to the listener's five senses. This imagery gives the listener the ability to paint a mental picture of the events in the story.

Transitional Phrases

Using **connectives**, or words and phrases that bring two ideas together, helps the story flow freely. They allow you to establish the time, place, and "how" of events in the story. Examples of connectives which indicate when an event takes place would be: once upon a time, a long time ago, shortly afterward and before. Connectives which describe where important elements of the story take place are: around the corner, a little farther, in the distance, as close as could be and just beyond. Vividly expressing "how" something takes place in a story is encouraged by using phrases that connect, such as: all of a sudden, excitedly, in the blink of an eye, before you knew it, and as fast as he could. These transitional phrases and words will hook the audience and keep them engaged in your story.

The Importance of Setting

When the story takes place and where the events happen provides for the **setting**. The time and place of a story is usually revealed through description. The setting can be presented in such detail as to conjure up clear representative imagery. Never underestimate the power of descriptive imagery when reciting words which describe the setting. The more the listeners know about the whereabouts of the action and characters, the better they will be able to visualize the setting in their imaginations.

The Importance of Mood

Establishing an emotional feeling about a story is called a **mood**. It is important for you to create a certain impression or evoke a response from the listener. Your story could require a mysterious, mystical mood, or it might hope to provoke a happier, humorous sensation. A gloomy, dreary mood may be important as the listeners prepare to hear a sad tale. Through the careful combination of dialog, description, setting, plot, and characters, the storyteller is able to bring about the suitable mood of a story.

As you choose a story to tell for a specific occasion, be sure to choose one with merit. The story should be one that you like. It should also be appropriate for the occasion and the audience. Think to yourself, "What do I like about this story?" The chances are that the audience will enjoy the story for the same reasons. As you become involved in the event of storytelling, so will your audience. As you display enthusiasm and a high energy level, you will generate their involvement and excitement about the story. Just remember that your intense attitude and ardent participation in the presentation of your story will have a tremendous effect on your listeners. You and your audience can share the enjoyment and thrill of the storytelling experience.

Don't Be Afraid to Express Yourself

Here are a few final pointers to assure the successful delivery of your story. If your story has several characters, change your voice to distinguish the characters' voices as you deliver dialog. Vary your physical posture, facial expressions and gestures to characterize the people involved in your story. Use direct audience eye contact to keep your listeners actively involved in your narrative. Be uninhibited as you relate a series of colorful events. Don't be afraid to express yourself. Let your tempo convey action and emotion. Exercise a variety of pace as you make interesting and appropriate changes. Know your story, but never memorize it word for word. Special parts may need to be memorized for a certain effect, but complete memorization could be disastrous. Last, but not least, relax and enjoy as you share yourself with your audience. Storytelling is a worthwhile endeavor which can be a thoroughly delightful experience for all.

There are a variety of storytelling activities which will provide you with the opportunity to apply the many ideas discussed in this chapter.

The Anecdote Exchange

Since a casual exchange of happenings and events takes place daily in our lives, the first activity is the anecdote exchange. In a small group circle made up of five or six members, each participant will relate a short story. The speaker should try to incorporate as many of the storytelling techniques as possible. This is meant to be a relaxed icebreaker. Have fun exchanging stories!

ACTIVITY — The Anecdote Exchange

OBJECTIVE

1. To promote good storytelling techniques through a brief story exchange.

INSTRUCTIONS

1. Get into small groups of five to six people.
2. Relate to your group a short entertaining story involving some happen-

---

ing or event in your life.

3. It should be suitable to you, your occasion and your audience.

4. An ending is especially important to an anecdote. Try to have a cleverly worded ending which ties up all loose ends.

5. Tell your anecdote effectively using good storytelling skills.

6. Show enthusiasm and interest as you recite your narrative.

Personal Experience Storytelling

After getting a taste of storytelling through the anecdote, you will be ready for the personal experience storytelling activity. This story involves plot development, details, suspense, dialog, movement and colorful language. Carefully plan your story prior to delivery. Remember to practice the story to familiarize yourself with the tempo and general flow of the story. The story may be any interesting event about yourself which you would like to re-create and relive for your audience. It doesn't have to be spectacular or earth-shattering. It can be a simple slice from your everyday life which you feel has potential for being a good story. How you tell the story will determine the audience response.

ACTIVITY — Personal Experience Storytelling

O B J E C T I V E

1. To promote good storytelling techniques through a personal experience speech.

I N S T R U C T I O N S

1. Prepare and tell a story which is a personal experience in your life.

2. Make the descriptions of the characters and setting as vivid as possible.

3. Use colorful, descriptive language.

4. Use details to help create the entire picture.

5. Use dialog.

6. Build to the climax or high point of interest in the story.

7. Be animated, movement adds interest.

8. Have vocal variety, especially show distinction with characters' lines or voices.

9. Use connectives effectively.

10. Maintain good eye contact throughout delivery.

Topic Suggestions

1. memorable vacation
2. water skiing
3. snow skiing
4. swimming or diving incident
5. sports event
6. audition or tryout
7. shopping trip
8. cooking experience
9. hospital stay
10. school day experience
11. dream

12. party
13. pet story
14. family crisis
15. restaurant scene
16. a dating experience
17. lessons of some kind
18. recital
19. performance
20. personal injury
21. baby-sitting
22. holiday

The Most Embarrassing Moment Speech

Another personal experience speech idea which specializes in an emotional display is the most embarrassing moment speech. Certainly everyone has experienced an awkward time of self-conscious distress. Time is a great healer of disconcerting incidents in our lives. It doesn't take long for us to be able to look back and laugh about that which we once thought humiliating. Remember you are just telling another personal story. Your success will rely on your ability to focus on the techniques and not the fact that this moment once made you uncomfortable.

ACTIVITY — The Most Embarrassing Moment Speech

O B J E C T I V E

1. To promote good storytelling techniques through the most embarrassing moment speech.

I N S T R U C T I O N S

1. Think of an embarrassing moment which you can tell in front of an audience.

2. Use details and play-by-play description of the plot in the incident.

3. Build to the climax of the story.

4. Don't just tell the story, create the entire picture.

5. Use movement and action to help tell the story.

6. Begin with an introduction which relates to your particular moment.

7. Give background information to lead into your story.

8. Use a conversational style in telling the story, as it will be humorous and entertaining.

Topic Suggestions

1. pants ripping
2. spilling drink or food
3. speaking in front of an audience
4. falling down
5. mistaken identity
6. sports error
7. swimming incident
8. driving disaster or lesson
9. date
10. slip of the tongue
11. falling off a horse
12. tripping
13. bumping into someone or something

You Were There

There are so many famous events in history which warrant being told. It's a shame we weren't there to witness those well-known moments in history. You can pretend you were either an active participant or an interested spectator. Tell about the event as if you were really there when it happened. Research the event to be sure of the specifics of that happening in history. Actually relive the historic moment and be creative as you add your own perspective to the telling of this event.

ACTIVITY — You Were There

OBJECTIVE

1. To promote good storytelling techniques through a "You Were There" speech.

INSTRUCTIONS

1. Prepare and tell some event in history which might be of particular interest to you and your audience.

2. The event should hold a substantial place in history.

3. Give a "bird's-eye-view" of the event as if you were an actual witness to or participant in the event.

4. You might use an event you have studied in history class as a possible topic.

5. Familiarize yourself with the event through research.

6. The speech will be told in first person.

7. No two people will be allowed to do the same event told by the same person. Two people may do the same event as long as it is told from a different person's point of view.

Topic Suggestions

Event	Person's Point of View
1. John F. Kennedy's assassination	Jacqueline Kennedy
2. First Thanksgiving	Pilgrim
3. Underground railroad	Harriet Tubman
4. Watergate	Richard Nixon
5. Bombing of Pearl Harbor	Serviceman
6. Sinking of the Titanic	Passenger
7. Discovery of America	Columbus
8. Invention of first airplane	Wilbur Wright
9. Signing of Declaration of Independence	Thomas Jefferson
10. First man on the moon	Neil Armstrong

Storytelling (Fairy Tale)

The lively re-creation of a fairy tale or fable is an entertaining pleasure for both storyteller and audience. Choose a title which you thoroughly enjoy and communicate your interest to the audience as you deliver the story. Remember your excitement will stimulate their interest. The storyteller must take time to prepare by reading the story aloud several times and then practicing many more times. Determine how long the story needs to be. Make necessary adjustments as you familiarize yourself with the plot and, especially, the high point of action. Acquaint yourself with the characters and develop voices and physical mannerisms for each.

A short introduction will serve to prepare your audience and set the mood for the presentation. It should simply reveal the title, author and a brief explanation of the story. Be animated. Facial expressions, physical actions, vocal variety, dialog and even costumes and props will enhance your performance. Your goal is to give life and vitality to your story.

ACTIVITY — Storytelling (Fairy Tale)

OBJECTIVE

1. To promote good storytelling techniques through the telling of a fairy tale or fable.

INSTRUCTIONS

1. Choose a fairy tale or fable.

2. Prepare and recite the story orally.

3. Develop distinct characters through physical movements, facial expressions, and vocal changes.

4. Use dialog as you tell the story.

5. Build the incidents in the story to the high point of action.

6. Get the audience's attention and set the mood with an introduction.

7. Use colorful, descriptive language.

8. Use connectives.

9. Use good eye contact.

10. Vary rate.

11. Use props, costumes, dolls, puppets, etc., to help you recreate the story.

12. Practice aloud several times.

Topic Suggestions

1. The Three Little Pigs
2. Goldilocks and the Three Bears
3. Hansel and Gretel
4. The Gingerbread Boy
5. The Princess and the Pea
6. Sleeping Beauty
7. Cinderella
8. Peter Rabbit
9. Alice in Wonderland
10. Rumplestiltskin
11. Little Red Riding Hood
12. Jack and the Beanstalk
13. Beauty and the Beast
14. Three Billy Goats Gruff
15. The Tortoise and the Hare

Original Fairy Tale

If you would like to try your hand at writing, the original fairy tale will be a challenging experience. This may be done individually or in small groups.

ACTIVITY — Original Fairy Tale

O B J E C T I V E S

1. To promote good storytelling techniques through the delivery of an original fairy tale.
2. To encourage creative writing.

I N S T R U C T I O N S

1. Write an original fairy tale, as an individual or in a small group.
2. Set the scene (castle, forest, etc.)
3. Choose and develop characters and animals.
4. Write dialog, narration and action into a script.
5. Read the story aloud *or* tell the story aloud *or* assign parts and present it as a play. You can divide parts and use one speaker as the narrator. Use props and simple costumes to help illustrate your story.

Modern Storytelling

Another fun way to incorporate creative writing skills and good storytelling techniques is through modern storytelling. This activity can be done very effectively as a group activity.

ACTIVITY — Modern Storytelling

O B J E C T I V E S

1. To promote good storytelling techniques through the delivery of a modern storytelling activity.
2. To encourage creative writing.

INSTRUCTIONS

1. Choose a story, a well-known fable or fairy tale.

2. Prepare one group script with narration, dialog, and action. Each group member should contribute ideas.

3. The majority of the script should be dialog, with minimal narration.

4. Use modern terms with setting, language, and characters.

5. The story should have the same basic plot as the original story. Do not deviate so much from the original version that the audience does not recognize the story or characters.

6. Assign the parts. Choose a narrator and evenly divide character roles among group members.

7. Develop strong characters through movement, voices, facial expressions, dialog and minimal props and costumes.

8. Parts should be memorized.

Creative Dramatics

The last activity in this chapter is an exhilarating group storytelling activity. This dramatic experience will excite participants and delight audience members. Everyone feels a part of the creative dramatics adventure. In small groups, you will skillfully act out a fairy tale. Action and characters' lines, along with a narrator's description, will provide a lively reenactment of a favorite narrative. Present your creative dramatics fairy tale as a short play. Polish and perform it for a children's group for fun. Play your part with much energy and enthusiasm, and your audience will thoroughly enjoy the presentation.

ACTIVITY — Creative Dramatics

O B J E C T I V E

1. To promote good storytelling techniques through a creative dramatics activity.

I N S T R U C T I O N S

1. The class will divide into small groups, approximately five people per group.

2. Choose a well-known fairy tale.

3. Simplify the story by deleting much of the description. Write a script with action, character lines, and narration.

4. Parts may need to be doubled up if there are many characters in the story.

5. Act out the fairy tale. It should be presented like a short play.

6. An introduction preceding the performance will include the name of the story and who will be playing the characters in the play.

7. Costumes, props and minimal settings will be used to aid the development and believability of the fable.

CHAPTER SIX

The Play's the Thing
Acting and Dramatics

Terms to Learn

pantomime
lip synchronization
props
blocking

run-through rehearsal
monolog
puppet

Acting is the most natural form of expression. We use our bodies and our voices to portray characters and situations to an audience. We use our entire bodies to communicate feeling and ideas. Actors rely on their bodies as well as their voices to reveal what they are thinking. You communicate the age of the character you are playing by making appropriate vocal changes and using a suggestive posture. The way a character walks can indicate certain personality characteristics. Body movement can give the audience vital information which is not revealed through dialog. The successful actor combines skills and knowledge to give a believable performance which captivates and stimulates each audience member.

Stage movement must be natural and lifelike. The actor strives to exhibit poise and control as he uses movements to communicate to the audience. If you are to be expressive as an actor, you must learn to use body action effectively.

Pantomime Is Dramatic Action Without Words

Pantomime is one form of acting which trains your body to demonstrate emotions, feelings, and attitudes through movement. Since you convey meanings, situations and characters through posture, facial expression and gestures, you learn the importance of expressive body movement. **Pantomime** is dramatic action without words. You do not speak or make sounds, you rely on movement alone.

Pantomime is not to be confused with mime work. Mimes use make-up, props, sound effects and costumes when performing a more stylized form of pantomime. In pantomime, the actor relies on his acting ability and creates the illusion in the minds of the audience members. If the actor successfully pantomimes the sounds, we *hear* them. If the actor successfully pantomimes his clothing, we *see* his hat, suspenders and pockets. This makes the art of pantomime a challenging experience. It also makes pantomime an acting activity which can be done anytime, anywhere. The actor needs nothing but an idea to turn the pantomime into a work of acting art.

Careful Planning Is Required for Effective Pantomime

There are several rules for successful pantomiming. You must organize your ideas. Pantomime is not simply movement. It must present a story with a beginning, middle and ending. The middle should be several clear movements which project and demonstrate precise meaning. Planning each step of your pantomime with definite detail will contribute to the clarity of your movement.

In addition to slow, exact bodily action, the actor must exaggerate all movements and facial expressions. In pantomime, you do not simply walk down the street. The movement must be heightened as you exhibit a character walking down the street. The face and body will demonstrate the situation and the emotions, age and personality of the character portrayed. The slight exaggeration brings the pantomime a step further than everyday movement and gestures. It becomes dramatic because you, as an actor, create expressive and vivid action which comes to life for the audience.

When planning your first pantomime, keep several things in mind. You must set your stage mentally. Determine how much space you need for your action. Decide where imaginary props, furniture and doors are. Make sure that they remain in the exact spot if they are immovable. You will break the illusion if the object loses its believability. Think about size, weight, shape and position of each object you use, and plan your movement accordingly.

Individual Pantomime

Visualize yourself as the character. Through your planned movement, let the audience see the character as you imagine him. Keep the action as simple as possible. The movements should be clear enough that the audience doesn't have to guess what is happening. Plan your movements with the audience in mind. It is important that even subtle facial expressions be visible to all audience members. Make sure movements are motivated and have reason. This will give definition to your pantomime. Concentrate on executing a single movement at a time to give the audience a focus and prevent stage movement clutter. Plan your introduction and conclusion carefully. Your introduction should arouse the interest in your scene and the conclusion should provide a definite ending to the character and situation.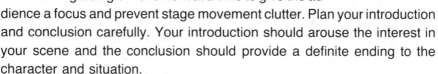

The first pantomime experience provided for in this chapter will be the individual pantomime.

ACTIVITY — Individual Pantomime

O B J E C T I V E

1. To develop the ability to create expressive body movement through pantomime.

INSTRUCTIONS

1. Choose an individual pantomime topic.
2. Work out a pantomime in steps.
3. Include an introduction, a body with clear, precise movements and an ending.
4. Use action, facial expressions, and posture to communicate a character and situation.
5. Exaggerate all actions and expressions.

6. No sound effects, costumes or props will be used.

7. Time limit is three to four minutes.

Topic Suggestions

1. watching a movie
2. baking a cake
3. going to a circus
4. eating an ice cream cone
5. making a pizza
6. sewing
7. eating at a restaurant
8. talking on the phone
9. washing a dog
10. directing traffic
11. setting the table
12. picking apples
13. cutting someone's hair
14. directing an orchestra
15. getting ready for school
16. walking a tightrope
17. catching a fish
18. decorating a Christmas tree
19. swatting flies
20. trying to mount a horse
21. riding a roller coaster
22. selecting a television show
23. buying a pair of shoes
24. hanging curtains
25. painting a building
26. driving a race car
27. watching a sports event
28. waiting in a dentist's office
29. burglarizing a home
30. reading a good book
31. taming a lion
32. roasting marshmallows
33. performing magic
34. walking a dog
35. ironing

Mirror, Mirror

The ideas for pantomime are endless! There are many pantomimes which work well with two or more people. One such pantomime which involves two people working together is the mirror pantomime. One person acts as if they are looking in the mirror while the other acts as the reflection. Movement for the mirror pantomime must be precise and synchronized. Be creative and original as you and your partner decide upon the movements in your pantomime. As with all pantomimes, this particular speech requires much practice.

ACTIVITY — Mirror, Mirror

O B J E C T I V E S

1. To develop clear precise pantomime movement through a partner mirror pantomime.
2. To develop interpersonal communication skills as you work with a partner.

I N S T R U C T I O N S

1. Get into pairs.
2. One person will be looking in the mirror, the other person will be the reflection.
3. Plan the pantomime step-by-step, down to the smallest detail.
4. Movements must be slow, precise and exactly together.
5. No talking, props, costumes or sound effects.
6. Practice several times for synchronization.
7. Time limit is one to two minutes.

[handwritten: Nathan, Jenna, Me]

Duet Pantomime

[handwritten: right up, left, both, scratch head, right kick, left kick, jump, r high, high]

There are many acting situations which work well for two people. Another partner pantomime which allows for interaction through movement is the duet pantomime. Two people work together to plan and present a scene. The rules which apply to the individual pantomime speech also apply to the duet pantomime. Combine talents and ideas as you develop a pantomime which is equally shared by both participants.

ACTIVITY — Duet Pantomime

O B J E C T I V E S

1. To develop the ability to create expressive body movement through duet pantomime.
2. To develop interpersonal skills through partner speech work.

INSTRUCTIONS

1. Get into pairs.
2. Plan a pantomime. Organize your ideas with a beginning, middle and ending.
3. Institute all rules of pantomime (no sound effects, no speaking, no props, no costumes, exaggerated movements, slow, precise action).
4. The scene should be equally shared by both people.
5. Time limit is four minutes.

Topic Suggestions

1. blind date
2. dentist's office
3. door-to-door salesperson
4. barber and customer
5. karate lesson
6. spectators at a sports event
7. a driving lesson
8. camping trip
9. cheaters on a test
10. teenager and parent argument
11. baby-sitting
12. decorating a Christmas tree
13. eating in a restaurant
14. a sport involving two participants, such as tennis
15. a dance lesson
16. washing a car

Group Pantomime

If working with a partner was an enjoyable experience, you will thoroughly enjoy group pantomime. Remember to be open-minded as you exchange ideas within your group. You might want to appoint or vote on a group leader to assure on-task organization. Taking a vote on major decisions also alleviates potential problems. You can feel a vital part of the group if you will contribute ideas during the planning stages of the pantomime.

A common error with group panto-mime performances is too much action at one time. The audience will become confused about where to focus if the body movement is not well planned. Organize step-by-step action. Every actor should know where he should be and what he should be doing during the entire pantomime. Acting and reacting should be taking place simultaneously.

ACTIVITY — Group Pantomime

O B J E C T I V E S

1. To develop the ability to create expressive body movement through group pantomime.
2. To develop interpersonal communication skills through group pantomime work.

I N S T R U C T I O N S

1. Get into groups of four to six people.

2. Work up a pantomime involving all group participants.

3. Remember all rules of pantomime.

4. Try to allow for equal sized parts.

5. A short, spoken introduction can be used to set the scene.

6. Time limit is four to five minutes.

Topic Suggestions

1. cafeteria food fight
2. students cheating on an exam
3. a dance class
4. a bank robbery
5. a bus ride
6. a game show
7. a trial
8. a fashion show
9. a traffic jam
10. baby-sitter with children
11. a hospital emergency
12. surgery
13. a wedding
14. double date
15. gun fight
16. highjacking a plane
17. group of teenagers getting stopped by police
18. an orchestra
19. a birthday party
20. spectators at a sports event
21. a concert
22. restaurant scene
23. gossiping neighbors
24. karate school

Guess Pantomime

Now that you have gained experience in several pantomime situations, you will be ready to test your skills. The next activity allows for the audience to view your pantomime and then guess what it is you are acting out. One fun way to use the guess pantomime activity is to work in groups of three actors.

Each group will choose one list of ten pantomime ideas. The group will go to the stage area and make sure each actor has adequate acting space. All three actors will simultaneously look at pantomime number one on the list and act out his/her idea for that pantomime. Hopefully, the audience will view three original and different ideas. The audience members will need paper and pen to record their guesses. The audience views all three pantomimes as the actors present their interpretation of the pantomime idea. This is not group pantomime, each actor is involved in an individual pantomime.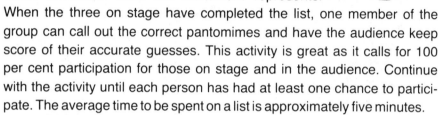

After watching each actor for a few moments, the audience should record a brief word or phrase which describes what the movement represents. When the three on stage have completed the list, one member of the group can call out the correct pantomimes and have the audience keep score of their accurate guesses. This activity is great as it calls for 100 per cent participation for those on stage and in the audience. Continue with the activity until each person has had at least one chance to participate. The average time to be spent on a list is approximately five minutes.

Creating a sequence of body movements without any prior knowledge of the scene characterizes this speech as impromptu pantomime. You must plan as you go. You will not be given time to prepare beforehand. Remember to apply the rules of good pantomime as you participate in this activity. The teacher or class leader can keep this activity moving by calling out the number for the next pantomime, after the audience has had ample time to guess the idea.

ACTIVITY — Guess Pantomime

OBJECTIVES

1. To develop the ability to create expressive body movement through guess pantomime.
2. To develop impromptu acting skills.

INSTRUCTIONS

1. Get into groups of three.
2. Select a list of pantomimes when your group takes its turn.
3. One group at a time will go to the stage area and act out all ten pantomime ideas, one at a time.

4. All actors pantomime #1, then #2, then #3 and so on.

5. Each actor does his/her own interpretation of each pantomime.

6. The audience studies all three people on stage and then records their guesses on paper.

7. Keep up with the number of correct guesses you receive.

List of Pantomimes
(Each list should be on a separate sheet of paper)

#1 Sports

1. bowling
2. Ping-Pong
3. weight lifting
4. ice skating
5. tennis
6. golf
7. basketball
8. body building
9. volleyball
10. water skiing

#2 Emotions

1. love
2. hate
3. surprise
4. doubt
5. embarrassment
6. fear
7. jealousy
8. sadness
9. pain
10. confusion

#3 Walk on These Things

1. squishy mud
2. hot pavement
3. slippery ice
4. burning sand
5. dry, crackling leaves
6. the moon
7. icy stream
8. sticky floor
9. thick foam rubber
10. shoes that are too small

#4 Animals

1. beaver
2. monkey
3. horse
4. bear
5. kangaroo
6. seal
7. wolf
8. crocodile
9. cat
10. rabbit

5 People

1. cashier
2. grandmother
3. salesperson
4. model
5. dog catcher
6. baseball pitcher
7. butler
8. beggar
9. burglar
10. spoiled child

6 People

1. boxer
2. energetic twirler
3. ghost
4. judge
5. baby-sitter
6. shoplifter
7. movie star
8. mad scientist
9. magician
10. barber

7 Holidays

1. Halloween
2. Thanksgiving
3. Valentine's Day
4. Easter
5. Memorial Day
6. April Fool's Day
7. 4th of July
8. New Year's Eve
9. New Year's Day
10. Christmas

8 Places

1. cemetery
2. bus
3. flower shop
4. pet store
5. amusement park
6. restaurant
7. toy store
8. dentist's office
9. elevator
10. shower

9 Songs

1. patriotic song
2. love song
3. Indian song
4. sad song
5. western song
6. opera
7. lullaby
8. Christmas carol
9. funny song
10. sea song

10 People

1. pianist
2. bank teller
3. tightrope walker
6. driving instructor
7. operator
8. fisherman

4. secretary

5. cheerleader

9. dog trainer

10. juggler

#11 Things You Feel

1. a slap

2. the rain

3. sticky tape

4. a pin

5. stubbed toe

6. frozen fingers

7. dirt in your eyes

8. mosquito bite

9. wind

10. bee sting

#12 Voice Sounds

1. cough

2. groan

3. sigh

4. sneeze

5. scream

6. snore

7. laugh

8. gulp

9. growl

10. cry

#13 Smells and Tastes

1. rotten eggs

2. roses

3. pizza

4. smoke

5. body odor

6. lemon

7. cotton candy

8. liver

9. hot coffee

10. gristle on meat

#14 Action Verbs

1. shopping

2. picking flowers

3. washing dishes

4. changing a flat tire

5. packing a suitcase

6. being shot

7. hunting

8. flirting

9. dancing

10. directing traffic

Lip Synchronization

Lip Synchronization is an activity in which actors pretend they are performing by moving their lips in time with a taped song or monolog. The performance really comes to life with choreographed stage movements and well-rehearsed pantomime.

The performer must first select original material. An actor might be tempted to choose his favorite current song, but this is not recommended. Humorous or mood material sometimes tends to work better for lip synchronization than the trendier hits. Explore the many varieties of music before making a selection.

Each participant chooses a song or monolog and learns the words to the selection. It is important that the song chosen be one in which the words are easily understood and learned. The lip sync must be executed with precision of lip movement and timing of cues in order to be believable. Exaggeration of lip movement helps create that look of believability. Facial expressions make every line come to life.

When performing the pantomime, you must create a strong character. Remember, you are acting. The lip sync is a performance, so strive to be believable. Work extra hard on timing so you come in on time with all cues. Nothing bothers the audience more than watching a person do a lip synchronization that is not planned properly. You cannot "fake it" on this assignment. Preparation and practice are extremely important. You won't regret the time and energy it takes to prepare an entertaining lip sync because this speech ranks as an audience all-time favorite!

ACTIVITY — Lip Synchronization

O B J E C T I V E

1. To develop the ability to create expressive body movement through the lip sync.

I N S T R U C T I O N S

1. Choose a selection from a tape or record.

2. Learn all the words.

3. Add movement or pantomimed action.

4. Exaggerate lip movement.

5. Add facial expressions.

6. Create a strong character.

7. Perform the selection using exact timing of cues.

---

8. Let the class be your audience.

9. Be uninhibited as you perform.

10. Microphones and costumes may or may not be used.

Music Pantomime

Along the same line as lip synchronization, but slightly different, is the music pantomime. The actor selects music with narrative lyrics and acts out the lines of the song. As the music plays in the background, the actor skillfully pantomimes the lyrics.

Music pantomime is another activity which uses music as a background for body movement. The actor does not use lip movement in music pantomime. You will instead act out the lyrics of the music you select. The lyrics must tell a story if you are to have styled action for each line of the song. This pantomime offers versatility as to the number of participants who can perform in a presentation. It depends upon the song you select. One song may need only one person, while another may require four people. Although group work can be fun, remember that it takes much organization and time to plan group practices.

This type of pantomime provides an excellent way to illustrate an important message. The universal appeal which music possesses allows this activity to have great audience attraction.

ACTIVITY — Music Pantomime

O B J E C T I V E

1. To develop the ability to create expressive body movement through music pantomime.

INSTRUCTIONS

1. Decide whether you would like to work solo or in a group.
2. Select your music.
3. Listen several times to the song and write down ideas for the pantomime.
4. Plan the music pantomime, creating line-by-line movement.
5. The movement should be synchronized with the lyrics of the songs.
6. Costumes and props may be used to enhance the performance.

Charades

Most people have participated in a game of charades at some time or another. It is actually a game of impromptu pantomime. The participants act out clues without speaking. There are many variations to this popular game, but dividing into teams creates a competitive spirit while encouraging expressive body movement. Charades works best when a group of rules is presented prior to the game. One impartial person should serve as timekeeper and scorekeeper. It's best to record the points where all players can see the score.

ACTIVITY — Charades

OBJECTIVES

1. To develop the ability to create expressive body movement in pantomime charades.
2. To promote participation through teamwork.

INSTRUCTIONS

1. Divide into two teams.
2. Select a team captain for each team.
3. The team captain receives titles and charade topics from group members. The titles may be in categories such as: songs, books, television shows or movies.
4. Each group writes down 10 titles on 10 separate pieces of paper.

Give the team titles to the scorekeeper. Each team's titles should be kept in a separate hat or box to keep from being mixed with the other team's charade titles.

5. To begin, one team member takes a turn by drawing a title from the opposing team's hat. This team member will be player number 1 from team A. He acts out his title for team A, while team A tries to guess the title from the pantomime clues player 1 gives. Player 1 is given a certain time limit, such as two minutes. Team B knows all ten titles team A will be presenting, so team B members may not guess.

6. If player 1 is successful and team A guesses the title within the two-minute time limit, the scorekeeper records a point for team A. If player 1 is unsuccessful, no point is recorded.

7. It is now team B's turn. Player 2 from team B draws a title from those prepared by team A. He then acts out the title for team B. Team B tries to guess the title within the two-minute time limit. If successful, a point is recorded for team B. This continues until all titles are gone or until game time runs out.

8. Remember to devise a set of rules before beginning the game. Symbols for songs, books, TV shows, movies, "sounds like" words, small words, syllables, etc., must be decided upon.

9. Having a list of written guidelines posted somewhere in the room will keep the game pleasant and void of constant interruptions.

The Jingle

A pre-recorded tape or record does not always have to be used when an activity calls for music. You can always create your own music and lyrics. When you write your own song and use it in advertising to "hook" or interest a potential customer, you have created a jingle.

A jingle is a catchy advertising phrase or verse which is sung or put to music. It is designed with a clever tune or memorable wording in order to stay in the mind of the consumer. Marketing people are paid large amounts of money to create catchy slogans and jingles which will sell a particular product.

The jingle not only creates auditory appeal, but visual appeal, as well. Adding interesting action to the witty jingle will provide an advertising campaign that will surely sell your product. The jingle can be sung, or spoken rhythmically with background music. The movement can be a choreographed dance sequence or any planned action which coordinates with the spoken word.

The jingle is actually a commercial which is taken a step further with a more elaborate musical presentation. Concentrate on meaningful movement as you create an interesting jingle. It will be a collaborative effort as you will be working in small groups. You might wish to video-tape this fun assignment. Watching your own performance, as well as others, offers an educational opportunity for you to critique your performance.

ACTIVITY — The Jingle

O B J E C T I V E S

1. To develop the ability to create expressive body movement in the jingle.
2. To promote creative writing.
3. To promote group participation and interpersonal communication skills through work on a jingle.

INSTRUCTIONS

1. Get into small groups of three-five people.
2. Choose a particular product on the market (Pepsi, Charmin, Oscar Mayer).
3. Write a song which the company could legitimately use in its advertising campaign.
4. The jingle may have an established tune or a new original tune which you create.
5. All parts and participation in the commercial should be equal.
6. The jingle must include carefully planned movement.
7. The song may be spoken, sung or a combination of the two.
8. Practice the jingle several times to coordinate and synchronize all singing and movement.

Play Writing as a Group Activity

To write an entire play would take much time and energy. A short scene can be written in a relatively brief period of time and provide a similar experience. The scene must possess interesting characters, a plot which builds to a high point of interest, a clever ending and a setting.

First, you must visualize your characters and decide what they are going to do in the play. The dialog should reveal the relationships of the characters. The scene must be planned step by step, in outline form. Once you have a basic skeleton of a play, the drama will begin to take form as you write the action and dialog. This activity is meant to give you a taste of play writing and stage acting in its simplest form.

You are going to be working in small groups as you write an original introduction and scene. The introduction should give information as to what the scene is about, author, and title of the play. The scene should be equally shared by all actors. The subject matter should be suited to the occasion and audience. It can be either serious or funny.

As you write the dialog, be sure to include all pertinent stage action. Include with your script a list of **props**, all properties needed on stage for the action of the play. These can be smaller hand props, such as a briefcase or cigarette case, or larger objects known as stage props, such as furniture or draperies. A complete list of all costuming items should be presented with the script.

A drawing of the stage area denoting placement of all properties will help when you are ready to stage the play. Plan ahead of time and organize the technical aspects of your short presentation to enhance your performance and reduce the chance of error.

Prepare a neat hand written or typed copy of the script. Each actor should receive a copy to use for line memorization. When it is time to present the scene, bring all items needed for the scene. If your scene calls for a living room setting, be creative with what's available and what you can easily bring. Don't overdo it by trying to prepare an elaborate set. Your acting experience should be the main focus for this activity. You will memorize the script and present the scene in front of an audience. Arranging for an audience to be present is a simple process. People love to watch creative talent at work. Having an audience tends to encourage a more polished product. Knowing others will be viewing your attempt at writing and acting causes your ego to take over. You want to experience success and have pride in your work, and you push yourself to achieve it.

Once you have a completed script, you are ready to work on **blocking**, the established stage movement of a play. Determine when a character enters and exits and what action he has while on stage. Establish curtain and lighting cues and include them in the **run-through rehearsals**. This means the actors perform an entire scene without interruptions. Establish characterization as you develop mannerisms, posture and facial expressions suitable for your character. Vocal flexibility should show variation in inflection, pitch, rate and volume. Try to achieve ensemble work as you share your scene and interact with the other characters.

Stage Movement

Play production is an extremely involved process. It is an entire course of study in itself. This activity will "get your feet wet" as you have a brief theatrical experience. You will need to know a few things about basic stage movement in order to present a successful production. Keep these ideas in mind as you prepare and present your scene.

Movement should have a purpose. When moving on stage, cross in front of characters and furniture, when convenient. When speaking to a character on stage, partially face the character and partially face the audience. Conversation should take place close to center stage, unless a reason exists for it to take place elsewhere. A character who is crossed should counter-cross to balance the stage. Generally speaking, move only on your lines. Too much movement and dialog will create confusion as to where the audience is to focus.

Don't allow yourself to be visible to the audience from any area offstage. Stand a few steps back from the side curtains when you plan an entrance. This will create a natural stride as you take the stage. The same principle holds true for exits, as well. Don't stop abruptly as you get to the side curtains, continue a few steps until you are completely out of sight. If you feel you need more information about stage movement, your instructor can easily offer reference materials or personal knowledge about stage grouping and correct stage blocking.

For a successful presentation, you should be aware of these play production reminders. Your back should not be turned to the audience, unless there is a specific reason for it. Be aware that your voice will be projected the direction you are facing. Articulate on stage as you speak with volume and crisp clarity. Never break character! You should never laugh out of character at yourself or another actor. Don't fade in and out of your character. Your character will lose believability! If you want the audience to believe in your character, you must avoid making direct eye contact with audience members. Unlike speech making, stage acting generally requires that you act as if there is no audience. If the audience laughs at a character's lines, hold for the laughter. Resume when the laughter begins to die down. You do this so that the audience will hear all lines. Make scene changes quickly. You don't want the audience to become restless as they sit and wait for another scene change. Do not upstage other characters or draw undue attention to yourself. Remember you are a team of actors. Don't just act out your lines and movements, but react to all character's and their lines, as well.

ACTIVITY — Play Writing as a Group Activity

O B J E C T I V E S

1. To encourage creative play writing.
2. To develop the ability to create expressive body movement on stage.
3. To develop stage acting skills.
4. To develop interpersonal communication skills while working in a group.

I N S T R U C T I O N S

1. Get into small groups of two-five people.

2. Write an introduction and a scene outline.

3. Use strong plot development as you outline the scene.

4. Write a script with all dialog and stage action.

5. The subject should be presentable and offer audience appeal.

6. The scene should be equally divided.

7. Write a list of all stage properties and costumes.

8. Draw a diagram of the stage setting.

9. Prepare a neat inked or typed script. Each actor should have a copy to

use for memorization.

10. Bring all items needed for the scene.

11. Memorize the script and present it in front of an audience.

Topic Suggestions

1. doctor's office
2. hijacking
3. hillbillies visiting city
4. trial
5. exercise class/dance class
6. roommates
7. time travel
8. bumbling burglars
9. a blind date
10. camping trip/camp
11. driving instructor and students
12. surgery/hospital stay
13. mad scientist and assistant
14. vacation
15. baby-sitting experience
16. bums, from rags to riches
17. murder mystery
18. old people in modern society

The Monolog

Learning to create a distinctive character takes much training. You try to visualize the character and every physical detail about him. You try to sculpt the portrait of your character as you reveal him to your audience. One way to accomplish this is through a cleverly worded monolog. A **monolog** is a dramatic selection where one person speaks in a conversation. We are able to know what other imaginary characters are saying by the reaction and response you give. If you use the pause effectively, the audience will be able to imagine the imaginary person. You deliver lines and movement as you create a scene or incident. Some scenes have only one actor's lines, while other monologs have characters who are revealed solely by the way the monologist delivers his lines and actions on stage.

ACTIVITY — The Monolog

O B J E C T I V E S

1. To encourage creative writing skills through the writing of a monolog.
2. To develop the ability to create expressive body movement on stage.

I N S T R U C T I O N S

1. Choose a character and incident about which to write.

2. This may be a scene with one person speaking, or it may involve two people conversing. The second person never speaks in the monolog. The lines are not actually written. The second character's lines are revealed only through the monologist's lines. Example — An operator talking to someone on the switchboard. "What was that you just said, Mr. Wagner? (pause) I'm as slow as *what*? (pause) If I'm as slow as Christmas, why don't you just wait until next December to call back!"

3. Write the entire monolog on paper. Concentrate on revealing character. Show how the person thinks and feels through the lines.

4. Memorize the monolog and add body movement and gestures.

5. Use vocal variety. Change your voice for the character, if appropriate.

6. Deliver the monolog to an audience.

7. Time limit is three-five minutes.

Topic Suggestions

1. a teenage girl waiting for a boy to call
2. a woman shopping
3. a girl dancing with a boy for the first time
4. an exercise instructor speaking to the class
5. a kindergarten teacher with his/her students
6. a telephone operator

86

7. an actor practicing an important scene
8. an inexperienced repairman
9. a psychiatrist with a patient
10. a dog taking a walk with his master
11. a monkey in a cage at the zoo
12. father speaking to dying son
13. a coach on the sidelines

The Game Show

Television includes such a variety of shows. One of the most popular of those is the game show. Some game shows test contestants' intelligence, while others offer a fun, competitive way to win cash and prizes. Most of us never have the opportunity to participate in our favorite game show, but we can have the next best thing — a parody of it. Since TV game shows are copyrighted as the property of the creators, you may not do a public performance using the exact same format of the show but you may do a "spoof" of it by slightly altering the names and procedures. You have seen this done on Saturday Night Live and other comedy shows. We can write a script which allows us to play game show hosts and contestants. What a fun speech activity! As with the monolog, you strive to create a believable character. The type of game show you choose will determine the amount of movement necessary for the play. Physical mannerisms and gestures will definitely be an important addition if the game show is to be believable.

ACTIVITY — The Game Show

O B J E C T I V E S

1. To encourage creative writing through the writing of a game show script.
2. To develop the ability to create a strong character on stage.
3. To develop stage acting skills.
4. To develop interpersonal communication skills while working in a group.

I N S T R U C T I O N S

1. Get into groups (the show you choose will determine how many people will be in a group).
2. Decide on a game show to parody.
3. Choose a role for each person to play.
4. Memorize your lines.
5. Perform the game show for class.
6. Props and costumes may be used.
7. Remember to create an interesting script.
8. Take time to prepare.
9. Make your script entertaining.
10. Be sure to be an equal contributor to the group.
11. No off-color words or distasteful ideas should be considered.

Topic Suggestions
(for a parody)

1. The Dating Game
2. The Newlywed Game
3. Family Feud
4. Jeopardy
5. Concentration
6. The 20-Thousand Dollar Pyramid
7. Love Connection
8. Match Game

9. Wheel of Fortune
10. To Tell the Truth
11. Win, Lose or Draw

The Puppet Play

The last activity to be discussed in this chapter is the puppet show. People of all ages are delighted by the lovable creatures which seem to come to life on stage. This activity can allow for a minimal amount of time and money to be invested in the project. Simple hand puppets made from socks and decorated with household objects require nothing more than creativity. A puppet stage can be constructed from a large cardboard box. Even curtains can be inexpensively and easily added to such a stage.

You have experience writing a play and creating a character. The puppet play gives you another opportunity for a play-writing experience. The major difference this time is that you will not be seen. You will remain behind the scene. Your puppet is the star of the show. Your job will be to learn to maneuver the puppet with control and meaning. A **puppet** is an animated figure which is controlled by a human. You can make the character as believable as you want by adding appropriate puppet movement as you deliver lines. You will also be responsible for creating an interesting character voice for your puppet. The script should possess strong plot development and provide for action. The plot should build step-by-step to a high point of interest. You will definitely captivate your audience with your puppet play if you supply an interesting script, use creativity as you produce the puppets representing the characters, and add vocal variety as you turn an inanimate piece of material into a believable, lively character.

ACTIVITY — The Puppet Play

O B J E C T I V E S

1. To encourage creative writing skills though puppet play writing.
2. To develop vocal variety.
3. To develop interpersonal communication skills through group work.

INSTRUCTIONS

1. Get into small groups of no more than four people.
2. Write a script using characters you can create as puppets.
3. Development of plot should allow for story action to build to a high point and then allow for unraveling action and a conclusion.
4. Make the puppets needed for the play.
5. Memorize lines for your characters. You will be busy maneuvering puppets and will not have a free hand to handle a script.
6. Prepare a stage to be used. The entire class can prepare one nice stage to be used for all puppet plays.
7. Present the puppet play to an audience. A group of children would thoroughly enjoy this type of dramatic presentation. Sharing your talents and hard work with others can be very rewarding.

This activity can also be done with a well-known story, fairy tale or fable. The puppets can be created for the characters in stories such as *Little Red Riding Hood, The Three Little Pigs,* or *The Tortoise and the Hare.* You will have to rewrite most stories to have less narration and more character lines. This can also be a very exciting and entertaining puppet play activity.

CHAPTER SEVEN

Is That a Fact?
Researched Speeches

Terms to Learn

research	*example*
testimony	*comparison*
fact	*contrast*
statistic	*triad*
illustration	*panel discussion*
narrative	

While speaking on those topics which you know about is clearly sound advice, learning to find and use new information in your various speaking occasions will give your ideas substance. Many speeches cannot stand alone, other sources of information are needed to support your knowledge of the subject.

To be most effective as a speaker, you will use materials from a combination of sources. You will use personal experience and knowledge, investigation, questioning, interviews and resources of printed materials. You read, discuss and observe as you prepare for a speech. Your curiosity and interest in a subject should be reinforced by disciplined study and thought. One source of ideas comes from personal investigation and the analysis you do following that investigation.

It is important for you to select a worthwhile subject and organize suitable materials. Learning to use all resources at your disposal will open yet another exciting door for you as a speaker. Research reading and analysis of the material will give you confidence as a speaker as you master a particular topic.

Research involves careful study and investigation for the purpose of gaining new knowledge. This collection of information about a subject provides you and your audience with insight and interesting ideas.

Interview Research

Conversation or interviews with knowledgeable people is another valuable source of information. Courses you are currently taking or have taken in the past can provide a wealth of ideas. Don't overlook the instructors with their experience and specialized knowledge of their subject area.

Local newspapers offer information on topics of interest within your community. Weekly and monthly magazines offer comments on the news on a much larger scope. The number of magazine types and their various subject matter is wide-ranged. These periodicals, published at regular intervals, will provide articles which offer viewpoints on contemporary issues. Books should not be forgotten as a challenging area for valuable research material. General reference books, such as encyclopedias, provide a good beginning for your research. The card catalog will assist you in locating specific titles and authors. Almanacs, atlases, dictionaries, and books of quotations give additional detailed support material for your speech topic.

Testimony Research

The research you include in your speech can either prove the accuracy of your statements or illustrate points of interest. The most common types of support are testimony, fact, statistic, narrative or illustration, example and comparison. You will clarify your statements with these types of verbal support as you obtain audience acceptance and understanding.

You may wish to cite another person's opinions to support your views. This **testimony** should come from an authority or expert in the field. By stating the person's name and special qualifications, the audience can be sure of the authority's specific expertise in the subject area.

Statistical Research

The strongest form of support, an event or a truth that has been observed or is known to exist, is the *fact*. A fact is an excellent example of support because it is not easily refuted.

Statistics, numbers which show comparison, are a useful form of support because of their accuracy. They are presented as facts which are stated in numerical terms, such as percentages or averages. Be sure to state the statistic in terms your audience can understand. Don't saturate your speech with too many statistics. Your audience will quickly tune-out if there are too many confusing numbers. Accuracy should be a concern as you select current statistics for use in your speech.

Examples and Comparisons

Using supporting material in the form of a story with a point will make your speech topic both interesting and enjoyable. This story, either real or imaginary, is called an *illustration*. It is also referred to as a *narrative*. The illustration is an invented story which allows the audience to suppose or imagine. These stories, depending upon your speech topic, may be either humorous or serious.

An *example* is a type of support where you state several specific facts or brief instances. These facts or statistics, narratives or testimonies support what you are describing in your speech. Your general statement becomes specific with examples.

A *comparison* points out the similarities between two unlike ideas to make them clearer to the audience. A *contrast* would show the differences between two dissimilar situations. Use these various types of support to prove the ideas you wish to express in your speech.

The Quotation Speech

The first speech activity will be a quotation speech. You will build a speech around someone else's words. You will choose a quote and use that particular idea as the nucleus of your speech. All other forms of support should be incorporated, when appropriate. Other quotes may be used to support or explain the chosen words about which you speak. The many books of quotations will help you as you make a selection for your speech topic. *Bartlett's Familiar Quotations* is an excellent source of quotable material.

ACTIVITY — The Quotation Speech

O B J E C T I V E S

1. To encourage the use and development of quotations within a speech.
2. To promote the use of research in speech writing.

I N S T R U C T I O N S

1. Locate a quote which interests you.
2. Develop a speech or speech outline about the quote, how it applies to you, what it means, the importance of it, illustrations and examples of it.
3. Use research to support and develop your speech ideas.
4. Try to use a wide variety of support such as: fact, statistic, narrative (or illustration), example, testimony, comparison, quotations.
5. Begin your speech with an introduction and summarize with a conclusion.

Topic Suggestions

1. No act of kindness, no matter how small, is ever wasted. — Aesop
2. Live and let live. — Scottish proverb
3. I never met a man I didn't like. — Will Rogers
4. That's one small step for man, one giant leap for mankind. — Neil Armstrong
5. There is no substitute for hard work. — Thomas Edison
6. I only regret I have but one life to lose for my country. — Nathan Hale
7. To thine own self be true. — Shakespeare
8. A journey of a thousand miles must begin with a single step. — Lao-tzu
9. I have regretted my speech, seldom my silence. — Livy
10. Union gives strength. — Aesop
11. The good befriend themselves. — Sophocles
12. Leave no stone unturned. — Euripedes

13. Men must trust their ears less than their eyes. — Herodotus

14. It's great to be great, but it's greater to be human. — Will Rogers

15. It is not fair to ask others what you are not willing to do yourself. — Eleanor Roosevelt

16. Keep your face to the sunshine and you cannot see the shadows. — Helen Keller

17. Don't let yesterday use up too much of today. — Will Rogers

18. A weed is but an unloved flower. — Ella Wheeler Wilcox

19. The man with the new idea is a crank until the idea succeeds. — Mark Twain

20. We must build a new world, a far better world. — Harry S. Truman

The Election Speech

Another type of speech which uses quotations as an anchor for speech development is the election speech. The quotation you chose will determine the direction of the your speech. This speech idea is practical and applicable as it provides for a true-to-life situation. You may at some time in your school career or life decide to run for an office. Knowing how to organize your thoughts and express yourself effectively is your ultimate goal as you make plans to run for an office. Even if you don't get elected, you personally know that you gave it your best shot.

ACTIVITY — The Election Speech

O B J E C T I V E S

1. To encourage the use and development of quotations within a speech.
2. To promote the use of research in speech writing.

I N S T R U C T I O N S

1. Choose an office for which you would like to run.
2. Locate an applicable quote and develop your speech around that particular quotation.
3. Use research to support and develop your idea.
4. Try to use a wide variety of support, such as: fact, statistic, narrative or illustration, example, testimony or comparison.
5. To begin your speech, first address your audience.
6. Next, introduce yourself.
7. State the office for which you are running.
8. Give past experience which demonstrates your leadership ability.
9. Tell your plans for the future. Don't make idle promises.
10. End with a short summary and a request for their vote.
11. In actuality, you would probably want to use the memorized style of delivery. For classroom practice, you may wish to use manuscript delivery.

The Current Event Speech

The next speech activity concentrates on periodical and newspaper research. To keep up with what is happening in the world, you must stay well versed on current events. You may be asked to report on current events in a history class. Knowing how to choose an appropriate topic and organize your ideas in order to present an interesting speech can prove very helpful. This speech should not be too lengthy. The purpose of the current event speech is to provide information about an important happening. One way to keep it short and on topic is to "weed out" the unnecessary information and only report that which is essential to the event. Many speakers choose to use the triad in speeches of this length. The *triad* is a speech technique in which the speaker relates three ideas. You might try to draw three important facts or ideas from your current event story. The audience will be able to focus and remember your three points of interest.

ACTIVITY — The Current Event Speech

O B J E C T I V E

1. To promote the use of research in speech writing.

I N S T R U C T I O N S

1. Bring material on ten current events.

2. The articles should be from either magazines or newspapers.

3. Choose one current event.

4. Outline the main ideas of the article.

5. Write a good introduction.

6. Conclude the speech.

7. Do not recopy the article, only pull from it the important ideas.

8. You may quote directly from the article, but the majority of your speech will be in your own words.

The Panel Discussion

The final activity in this chapter provides a method for problem solving through group discussion. The panel discussion is a speech topic which can be practically applied to everyday life. One of the best ways to reach a solution to a proposed problem is to talk about it. A *panel discussion* is a structured, formal discussion where a topic is explored by group members who sit before an audience. School, community, national and social issues all make excellent panel topics.

The Mechanics of a Panel Discussion

The panel is composed of a chairperson and two to six members. With several people working together, the group is able to work through more complex problems. The group discussions also allow for a variety of viewpoints and can provide an atmosphere for learning that an individual may not experience alone. Panel discussions give each person the chance to belong to a group and share the responsibilities of researching and reporting the information. The panel should be arranged so that group members can see the audience and be seen by the audience members. Each panel member speaks briefly several times throughout the informal discussion. The panelists do not speak from prepared speeches. They interact spontaneously and react to other group members' comments. To be able to communicate effectively, you will need to be well informed about your group topic. Many panel discussions require research. This research will allow the group members to discuss the problem, present all the facts and then arrive at a logical conclusion. Open-mindedness is necessary if you are to sift through the different materials and viewpoints and arrive at a logical solution within the group.

To begin the panel discussion, the chairperson will make a brief introduction in which a statement of the topic is made. The chairperson will introduce the panel members, giving names, titles, and areas of expertise. Relate to the audience the major issues to be discussed. With the audience members listening in, the panel members explore and analyze the topic. The members talk among themselves, sometimes focusing within the group, other times addressing the audience. When the problem has been adequately discussed, the chairperson calls for questions from the audience. The questions are followed by a brief summary. The chairperson thanks the panelists and the audience members for their participation in the panel discussion.

ACTIVITY — The Panel Discussion

O B J E C T I V E S

1. To promote the use of research in a group panel discussion.
2. To promote participation in a group project.
3. To develop extemporaneous speaking skills.

I N S T R U C T I O N S

1. Get into groups of three to seven people.

2. Choose a topic which interests your group members.

3. Elect one member as panel leader.

4. Spend two to three days researching your topic.

5. Meet with your group to organize and prepare for the presentation.

6. Note cards may be used during the presentation.

7. The group will assist the chairperson in preparation of introductory and closing remarks.

8. Each group will present a panel discussion of approximately 15 minutes.

9. A question period of 15 minutes will follow the panel's presentation.

Topic Suggestions

1. child abuse	21. patriotism
2. crime rate	22. school policies
3. energy	23. women's rights
4. the arms race	24. eating disorders
5. censorship	25. battered women's rights
6. prison reform	26. violence on TV
7. gun control	27. UFOs
8. racial discrimination	28. the court system
9. school spirit	29. capital punishment
10. school cliques	30. test tube babies
11. drug and alcohol abuse	31. suicide
12. ecology	32. pornography
13. smoking	33. runaways

14. violence in sports
15. gossip reporting
16. fads and fashions
17. divorce
18. teenage marriage
19. dating
20. teenage parents

34. missing persons
35. sexual harassment
36. advertising
37. reckless driving
38. sports figures' salaries
39. suggested age for voters

CHAPTER EIGHT

Instant Speech
Impromptu Speeches

Terms to Learn

improvisation
ad-lib

Having to speak before an audience without preparation has to be one of the most difficult situations for a beginning speaker. You are called upon to speak on the spur-of-the-moment, and you have no time to read about the subject or rehearse what you would like to say. There are certain situations where you may be asked to act out a scene without practice, script or time to learn lines. These speaking occasions sound terrifying, especially to beginning speakers, when actually they are exciting and can be quite fun. This type of instantaneous speaking involves activities, such as impromptu speeches and improvisational acting. Both types of activities give the speaker or actor an excellent opportunity of learning to create while doing. You learn to "think on your feet" as the speech or scene progresses.

When you are called upon to discuss a topic in a class or at a meeting, you will have only a brief moment to collect your thoughts before you begin to speak. You certainly do not want to be overcome with anxiety at the prospect of speaking without an outline, notes or prepared speech.

You will have many extremely embarrassing moments if you have trouble handling these brief impromptu speaking situations. To become more comfortable with the occasions which call for unprepared speech-making, you simply need the opportunity to practice. This type of speaking can be very beneficial as you become more efficient in organizing ideas when you speak. You will become a stronger speaker in day-to-day speaking situations. You will learn to speak about various subjects with confidence and ease.

The Impromptu Speech

When delivering the impromptu speech, you follow the basic speech organization rules. Begin the speech with an introduction which gets the audience's attention. Remember the rhetorical question, startler, quotation and personal story are among the many effective ways to begin a speech.

Lead into the body of your speech by telling the audience what you will be talking about. Stay on your topic. It's easy to get side-tracked in impromptu speaking since you don't know exactly what you are going to say next. Concentrate on making three major points. Discuss, describe, illustrate or elaborate on these main ideas. Speak from associations. What comes to mind when you first think of your topic? It could be a personal experience relating to the speech topic, or it may just be something you've heard or read which pertains to your subject. Describe your subject. Tell all you can about it, any details which have to do with your topic or your relationship to the topic. Do these things, but in an organized manner. Don't talk circles around your speech topic. Be direct, interesting and informative. Try to remain relaxed and self-confident as you translate thoughts into words through impromptu speech delivery.

ACTIVITY — The Impromptu Speech

O B J E C T I V E

1. To promote speaking without prior preparation through impromptu speaking.

I N S T R U C T I O N S

1. Using the speech topics listed or creating topics of your own, select three topics from a hat, box or envelope. The topics can be typed or hand written on a sheet of paper and then cut into smaller strips of paper. Each topic should be on a separate sheet of paper.

2. After looking at all three topics, select one about which you would like to speak.

3. Return the other topics to the hat for another speaker to have as a speech choice.

4. You will be given 30 seconds to prepare and gather your thoughts.

5. Speak for two minutes on your speech topic.

6. Try to organize your speech. Use an introduction, body and conclusion.

7. First, tell your audience what you are going to tell them. Second, tell them. Third, tell them again what you told them.

8. Keep your speech simple, concise and on topic.

9. Remember to organize your thoughts into major ideas and explain each main point.

10. The speech length can increase as the speaker gains experience in impromptu speaking.

Impromptu speaking can be done with more time taken for preparation and longer speaking time limits. For example, two to three minutes may be taken to prepare, and the speech length may be increased to five or six minutes. Generally, the topics used for two-minute speeches are single words. With a longer length speech, more difficult topics could be used. Well-known cliches or phrases, current events or famous quotes could provide possible speech topics. The important thing to remember when making a list of suggested topics is to keep the practice topics simple.

Choose topics that most people could speak about knowledgeably. Don't pick topics which are complicated or overly technical. This type of speech is difficult enough without adding complex subjects to embarrass the speaker and confuse the audience.

Topic Suggestions I

1. telephone	30. candy bar	59. divorce
2. gorilla	31. mustaches	60. books
3. feet	32. babies	61. motorcycles
4. parents	33. chicken	62. football
5. balloons	34. cars	63. fire
6. anger	35. dog	64. cowboys
7. scary movies	36. popcorn	65. pigs
8. ESP	37. clowns	66. college
9. ghosts	38. meatloaf	67. president
10. sadness	39. dancing	68. dolls
11. dentists	40. frogs	69. monkey
12. bananas	41. flirting	70. mugger
13. mathematics	42. school	71. belly dancing
14. teachers	43. hamburgers	72. death
15. ears	44. cows	73. bumblebee
16. movie stars	45. tails	74. bald heads
17. terrorism	46. suicide	75. boys
18. love	47. buses	76. cheating
19. athletes	48. girls	77. politics
20. dating	49. tornado	78. elem. school
21. violence	50. dates	79. vandalism
22. gum	51. buttons	80. science
23. English	52. happiness	81. women
24. government	53. bandanna	82. prison
25. baseball	54. child abuse	83. cats
26. ice cream	55. men	84. painting
27. crime	56. teeth	85. fast food
28. basketball	57. soccer	86. exercise
29. drugs	58. toes	87. families

Topic Suggestions II

1. Save Mother Earth.
2. Blood is thicker than water.
3. Count your blessings.
4. Two heads are better than one.
5. Practice what you preach.
6. Forgive and forget.
7. America, love it or leave it.
8. Never put off until tomorrow what you can do today.
9. All work and no play makes Jack a dull boy.
10. Slow, but sure.
11. Beauty is only skin deep.
12. Beauty is in the eye of the beholder.
13. Easier said than done.
14. Being a true friend takes a lifetime.
15. You have to believe in yourself to succeed.
16. Happiness begins at home.
17. Follow the beat of a different drummer.
18. Take the road less traveled.
19. No pain, no gain.
20. Don't put all your eggs in one basket.
21. The longest journey begins with a single step.
22. Brother helped by brother is a fortress.
23. The most important things aren't things.
24. No guts, no glory.
25. Honesty is the best policy.
26. An apple a day keeps the doctor away.
27. Early to bed — early to rise — keeps a man healthy, wealthy, and wise.
28. United we stand, divided we fall.
29. Do unto others as you would have them do unto you.
30. People who live in glass houses should throw no stones.
31. Patience is a virtue.
32. Silence is golden.

Improvisation

Learning to speak without prior preparation takes much concentration. You learn to focus and organize ideas as you go. Improvisation is a similar activity in that you create dialog and movement as you act out a scene. You have no definite lines to learn or scripts to follow. Your scene develops as you creatively think on your feet. Your lines come as you play off of the other actors. All actors contribute to the development of the scene.

Essentials in Building a Scene

The first thing you will need is an assortment of scenes from which to choose. You can formulate ideas individually or in small groups. Think to yourself, *who* are the characters? *Where* will the action take place? *What* is happening? If the actors have this information, a scene can develop. Actors can use this information to create strong characters with interesting lines. Never determine *how* the scene will develop. This is what makes improvisation a spontaneous acting experience.

It is vitally important for an improvisational actor to continually contribute to the scene, both through words and actions. Don't rely on the other actors to keep the scene going. You share the responsibility of keeping the scene alive with the other actors. Get involved and try to let the scene flow naturally. Think about how your character should react to the other characters and their lines. Use vocal qualities, gestures and posture to enhance your characterization.

If you will work towards a focal point, your scene will have direction. Direct your powers and energy toward that end result. Don't worry about making a fool of yourself. Do your own thing, try to find your own special way. Avoid copying the style of other actors. Believe in what you are doing and do it believably. Your stage movements and lines are equally important. You won't be able to have all the props that you need, so try to create them through pantomime.

Try to create a spirit of camaraderie as you work together. You are not competing, but contributing as a valuable group member. Don't be guilty of "hogging" the scene. This upstaging can destroy the scene and keep the other actors from contributing.

The scene length depends on the type of improvisation you are doing. Generally, improvisations last one to five minutes. Actors should always try to end the scene when they feel they have given the scene ample time to develop completely.

ACTIVITY — Improvisation

O B J E C T I V E

1. To develop impromptu or improvisational acting skills.

I N S T R U C T I O N S

1. Using the improvisations listed or creating topics of your own, select a topic.
2. Select other actors, as needed, to perform in the scene.
3. Go to the stage area and prepare for the scene with any available stage furniture or props.
4. You will have 30 seconds to prepare. This time is basically used for finding your place on stage and determining who will begin the scene. There should be no prior discussion of how to play or end the scene.
5. Time limit will be determined according to the type of topics used (1-5 minutes).
6. Look for possible openings of which you can take advantage and add to the dialog and development of the scene.
7. Continue to improvise the scene without stoppng until you reach a point where you can successfully end the scene.

Topic Suggestions

1. an eccentric interior decorator with a conservative client
2. a cocktail party of high society people
3. a group of novice campers
4. parents' discussion with teenager
5. astronauts meet aliens

6. group of people stranded in an elevator
7. a kindergarten class with teacher
8. a murder trial
9. bumbling burglars
10. disturbed person on window ledge threatening to jump and people trying to intercept
11. a hospital emergency
12. game show with host and contestants
13. a burning building with trapped people and firemen
14. a highjacking of an airplane
15. style show
16. swimsuit competition
17. discount department store shopping
18. visit to the zoo
19. pet store with customer and animals
20. baby-sitting with baby, mother and sitter
21. country and western song writers' competition
22. bomb threat
23. soap opera
24. family at an amusement park
25. restaurant scene
26. golf game with different level players
27. performer backstage with fans
28. beach scene
29. a newscast
30. a blind date
31. a dance class with instructor
32. automobile accident
33. women's beauty shop

Freeze Improvisation

A variation of the improvisation activity in which both stage actors and audience members actively participate is freeze improvisation. The audience members determine the scenes played on stage. A beginning scene is introduced by the teacher or group leader. For example, five actors go to stage area to perform a highjacking of an airplane. When they have been given at least two to three minutes to develop the scene, an audience member may interrupt the stage action by calling out the word "freeze." All actors on stage freeze in place immediately. The audience member then goes to the stage and takes the place of an actor (including the frozen physical position), and begins dialog for a new scene. All actors on stage respond accordingly. The new scene continues until another audience member "freezes" the scene, takes his/her place on stage and begins another new scene.

You can see how the audience members must stay involved with what's going on with the stage performers. Audience participation and involvement is the key to the success of this activity. An audience member sees the potential for a new idea to develop from what is taking place with the actors and responds immediately to stop the scene and freeze the actors in place. This activity challenges the actor as it provides for participation in a collage of acting experiences in a brief period of time. What a fun way to learn to *ad-lib*!

The unwritten lines which are composed as the actor performs can empower the actor with great confidence. Stage fright is lessened because the actor knows he will not be "at a loss for words" should his memory fail him. Your ad-lib or improvisational acting skills can really pay off when you become involved in full length stage work.

You will learn that if a problem presents itself during a production, all is not lost. You can improvise your way through the rough spot; and, chances are, your audience will never be aware that a problem existed.

During freeze improvisation, any actor who wishes to be on stage stays involved by watching for a chance to freeze the scene. He/she then receives an opportunity to test his/her acting abilities. This spontaneous activity is a definite favorite for all.

ACTIVITY — Freeze Improvisation

O B J E C T I V E

1. To develop impromptu or improvisational acting skills.

109

INSTRUCTIONS

1. The leader or teacher selects a group of actors.

2. The actors are given a scene. (More details may be given for the opening scene, such as: who, what, where).

3. The actors get thirty seconds to prepare and get into place on stage.

4. The actors are given at least two to three minutes to develop the scene.

5. Audience members think of potential scene ideas and prepare to "freeze" the scene.

6. As an actor freezes the scene, he takes the place of any actor on stage.

7. The new actor changes the scene idea and has the responsibility of beginning the scene.

8. This continues with audience participation as long as time allows.

9. Always allow ample time for the scene to develop before changing to a new scene.

Expression of emotion is a vital part of any actor's portrayal on stage. The emotions motivate the actor into action. An improvisational activity which encourages the expression of emotions while developing concentration is the argument improvisation.

Argument Improvisation

You and a partner are given a situation which stimulates the emotions. The conflict of interests from both sides of the argument should be evident. You are to appear strongly opinionated and determined as you defend your position on the issue. Reveal your emotions through use of voice and body movements as you try to communicate every possible argument. Do not let up, create new and more convincing arguments as you build the scene.

ACTIVITY — Argument Improvisation

O B J E C T I V E S

1. To develop concentration through argument improvisation.
2. To encourage and develop the ability to express emotions and opinions through improvisation.

I N S T R U C T I O N S

1. Get a partner with which to work.
2. Select a situation which will create a conflict.
3. Decide who will begin the argument.
4. Discuss only who you are in the scene, what is happening, and who will begin. Do not discuss anything else about the scene.
5. Do not give in. Be as strong as you possibly can as you defend your side of the argument.
6. Don't be afraid to express emotion. Get involved physically and vocally.
7. Time limit is three minutes.

Topic Suggestions

1. teenager and parent argue about attending a party.
2. store manager and customer argue over prices.
3. husband and wife argue about a financial matter.
4. cab driver and passenger argue about directions.
5. waiter and patron in restaurant argue about an order.
6. two small children argue over a toy.
7. two customers argue over the last sale item.
8. two roommates argue over arrangement of furniture.
9. two mothers argue over their children's talents.
10. two drivers argue over an accident.
11. two lawyers argue over a case.
12. dissatisfied customer and complaints department manager argue about a product.
13. boy and girl argue about date plans.

Talk Show Improvisation

Once you "get your feet wet" with improvisation, you won't want to stop impromptu performing. It is an exciting activity which offers much fun as you learn.

Another improvisational situation which provides limitless possibilities for creative acting is the improvisation talk show. Everyone has seen a talk show, such as *The Tonight Show,* starring Johnny Carson. The host has a variety of guests and conducts a live impromptu interview with each celebrity. Some celebrities perform prior to their interviews. Others simply discuss their lives, jobs, current and future interests.

There are several recommendations for this type of improvisation. The host must continue questioning and keep the show going no matter what response he gets from a guest.

A new guest can easily be introduced to bring life to a dying scene. If you are playing a guest, part of the fun is not knowing who you will be until the introduction from the host. Talk about spontaneous! You will have a split second to get into character as you make your stage entrance. This activity forces your brain to use imagination and stored information resources as you are called upon to perform or answer interview questions in character.

As you answer, refrain from using "yes" or "no" responses. Your host will become frustrated and uneasy if he is forced to rapid-fire questions because of your minimal responses. Elaborate and explain as you answer questions. If you have an idea for a line of questioning, give a subtle hint to your host. Hopefully, the host will take note and lead his next group of questions in that direction.

ACTIVITY — Talk Show Improvisation

O B J E C T I V E S

1. To develop impromptu or improvisational acting skills.
2. To develop interviewing skills.

INSTRUCTIONS

1. Choose a host and several people to be guests on the talk show.

2. Set the stage in a talk show arrangement.

3. The host begins the activity with an overall introduction. He/she then introduces the first guest.

4. The first guest assumes the character named and participates in an interview with the host.

5. Each guest is brought on stage one at a time.

6. Guests may or may not remain on stage after the interview to add additional comments to the following guest's appearance.

7. The host will determine the length of each individual interview.

8. When all guests have been interviewed, the host concludes the talk show.

CHAPTER NINE

Bring Literature to Life

Oral Reading

Terms to Learn

oral interpretation
literature
prose
fiction
nonfiction
poetry
narrative poetry
lyric poetry
universal appeal
fictional or dramatic speaker
denotative meaning

connotative meaning
simile
metaphor
personification
onomatopoeia
figurative language
assonance
alliteration
transition
readers theatre
suggestion

You can probably remember someone reading to you in your child-hood. It could have been an older sibling, a parent or a teacher who read aloud a favorite story. Good oral readers have a way of transforming an author's written words into spoken sounds while providing great insight into the literature. *Oral interpretation* is the performing of literature aloud for an audience to communicate meaning. It is an enlightening way to share the wonderful world of literature with other people.

Oral Interpretation

Literature is written material of lasting and widespread interest. When choosing your oral reading material, you must learn to distinguish what is worthy of interpretation. By carefully analyzing the material, you will develop an understanding of literature with merit. You learn to read carefully and look for the meaning in literature as you prepare for a performance. The audience benefits as they see the literature come to life. It is an enjoyable and valuable activity for both speaker and listener.

Many Types of Literature for Oral Interpretation

There are many types of literature which can be used for oral interpretation. The two major categories of literature are prose and poetry. **Prose** is the ordinary language that people use when they speak or write. The two types of prose are fiction and nonfiction. **Fiction** is material created in the imagination. The made-up story has imaginary characters and events. Novels and short stories fall into the fiction category. **Nonfiction** writing is literature about real people and actual events. Diaries, personal essays, biographies and autobiographies make up a majority of nonfiction literature.

Poetry is writing chosen and arranged to create a certain emotional response through meaning, sound or rhythm. Two major types of poetry which interpreters often perform are narrative and lyric poetry. **Narrative poetry** tells a story, while **lyric poetry** expresses feelings, thought and emotions.

Oral Interpretation Is Not Public Speaking or Acting

It is important to emphasize that oral interpretation is neither public speaking nor acting. Public speakers prepare speeches, writing and researching ideas they wish to express. Rarely are you the author of the literature you perform in oral interpretation. You, as interpreter, are the connection between the written word and the audience. You attempt to create the meaning in the minds of the audience. You do not memorize lines and assume the role of a character. You will always have the literature with you. You do use your voice and body to suggest the characters as you work to give meaning to the literature. Interpretation is not simply reading aloud from a book or manuscript. You go a step further as you carefully study, prepare and rehearse your selection. It is your responsibility to communicate as clearly as possible the author's intent. Your goal is to bring the literature to life.

Choice of Material Is Important

The first thing you must do is choose the right selection. Think about your likes, what the audience would appreciate, and the occasion and purpose of performing. They are all important considerations in choosing material for oral interpretation. Choose material you find appealing as you select your literature. Determine what would be interesting to you. You will be spending much time and energy working on the material you choose, so it is wise to take time to find literature with which you feel a strong connection. You will be able to share your enthusiasm with the audience members and feel more successful in delivering your selection if you genuinely like what you are interpreting.

Consider Your Audience

The audience should be a factor as you make your selection of literature. After all, you want the audience to get involved with the reading and feel a connection with the literature, as well. You want the literature and the way it is presented to excite the listeners and stimulate their imaginations. Can the literature be enjoyed by many different types of people? Does the material deal with experiences with which most people easily identify? Material with a common theme, such as love or loneliness, is said to have **universal appeal.** It is a good idea to choose a work which appeals to almost any type of audience. They will be able to appreciate the literature without possessing any specific knowledge.

Consider the Occasion

The occasion and purpose can make a difference in the type of material you perform. Consider what your speaking situation involves. Analyze the situation prior to the performance to determine the time limit, the age and number of audience members and the exact reason for your performance.

Once you have chosen a piece of literature, you will begin to analyze the selection to discover its full meaning. There are many factors to consider as you go through a process of understanding the literature. First, read the selection several times to get a feel for the literature. Determine who is speaking. It might be the author, or it could be a character created by the author. This **fictional or dramatic speaker** is the voice you hear telling the story. You should strive to speak and behave as the dramatic speaker in the story as you present your oral presentation.

Denotative and Connotative Word Meanings

As you continue with your read-throughs, you should be sure to check the meanings and pronunciations of unfamiliar words. The author chose the words carefully as he/she tried to express a feeling or thought. Consider both the denotative and connotative meanings as you prepare the selection. **Denotative meanings** deal with the literal or dictionary meaning of a word. A **connotative meaning,** an implied meaning of a word, deals with an emotional or personal response to a word. That which comes to mind when you hear the word, the meaning you attach to the word, is connotative meaning. You should read from your own personal experience because those experiences will give understanding to the printed word. Both types of meaning are essential for you to understand as an interpreter if you are to truly communicate the meaning of the literature.

Similies, Metaphors, Personification and Onomatopoeia

Many authors use figures of speech, such as similes, metaphors, personification and onomatopoeia. A **simile** is a comparison between two things that are similar. The words *like* and *as* are used to connect the two similar objects. "Your life is like a burning candle" is an example of a simile. A **metaphor** is a direct, implied comparison. It omits the words, *like* or *as*. "She was a spider, cautiously weaving her web." **Personification** gives human attributes to an inanimate object or abstract idea. "The mountain hears the silence and echoes her loneliness." An **onomatopoeia** uses words that imitate natural sounds. "Boom," "hiss," "pop," "quack," "crash," "boing," and "smack" are all words which sound like their meanings. **Figurative language** — simile, metaphor, personification and onomatopoeia — explains and modifies ideas as it makes ideas more vivid and alive.

As you analyze your selection, look at other literary elements, such as plot, setting, theme, mood and characters. Not all literature possesses these elements, but you should study them if you hope to convey the meaning of the literature.

Essentials for Creating a Mood

The plot, or important events which move the story along, needs to be studied in oral reading selections. You must understand the high points of action in order to communicate them to the audience. Knowledge of the setting is essential if you are to allow the audience to visualize the time and place of the action. Create a mood which sets the emotional feeling for the literature. Your verbal delivery and physical nonverbal communication both play a major part in your establishing an appropriate mood.

Characterization

Determining and understanding characters and their entire make-up will enhance your performance. In order to successfully suggest the characters' appearance, attitudes, vocal qualities and actions, an interpreter must take a close look at the characters involved in the reading. Get to know them, and you will be able to believably and naturally portray them.

Working Within Time Limitations

Once you have selected your literature and analyzed the material, you will want to cut the selection to meet the time limit for the oral interpretation. This means lifting the desired section from a longer literary work without altering the meaning of the selection. Combining several shorter pieces of literature is another option for oral interpretation. The collection should have a common characteristic which ties the pieces together, such as theme, topic or author.

With the cutting or collection chosen, you are now ready to prepare the selection for presentation. There are a number of things you must do before you will have a manuscript ready for practice. You must mark the manuscript to assure the best possible reading.

Underline the important words you want to stress.

example: Is he a _**purple**_ monster

Who eats _**normal**_ people?

Or is he a _**normal**_ monster

Who eats _**purple**_ people?

Draw arrows to show placement of characters' voices.

> **example:**   And when I yell,
>
> "I gotta go!"
>
> She says, ↗ "I'll be out soon."

As you read the character's lines, you look in the direction of the arrow. The physical movement, along with a vocal change for the character's voice, will help the audience distinguish between two or more characters.

Indicate gestures or vocal changes by a word or phrase in parentheses.

> **example:**   Hey — where did he go? (look around, show surprise)
>
> To the show? (disappointed)
>
> Oh. (sadly)

Assonance and Alliteration

When poetry uses **assonance,** the repetition of a vowel sound, you will want to place emphasis on these lines. You will do this by circling the important sounds you want to articulate.

> **example:**   A gummy girl named Glenda Sue — alliteration
>
> She oozed her glues on lots of shoes — assonance

Add any other helpful hints to your manuscript which will allow your delivery to move from a plain, non-energetic, first reading to an enthusiastic, polished performance. To show you would like to pause, use a diagonal line. A single line would call for a short pause, while more lines would indicate a longer pause is needed.

> **example:**   I got the day right, / the fourteenth, /
>
> But wrong month, / / / January !

To ensure that a line or phrase be read without stopping, use a curved line under the phrase.

> **example:**   Fun-filled sensation,
>
> A yearly vacation.

An arrow at the end of a line designates the continuation of a thought without a pause.

example: Words, "Enter at your own risk" should →

Be posted on the doorway wood.

When an increase in the rate is needed, a broken line is used.

example: And somehow know I'll be alright. / / /

Goodnight.

With your manuscript marked for practice, you now prepare an introduction for your literature. You already know the importance of the introduction. It serves a vital function in oral interpretation. You will want to get the attention of the audience and prepare them for the reading. Your audience is depending on you to provide the background information they need in order to enjoy the literature. Tell your audience the title of your selection and information about the author. Include a brief explanation of the piece, explaining characters and plot leading up to the cutting. The introduction must be brief, to the point, and presented in a natural style.

If you put together several poems or short excerpts in one presentation, you will want to link the pieces together with a *transition.* A brief line of explanation may be used to bridge the two selections, or a lengthier explanation might be used to give adequate information for a clear understanding of the new literature.

The Importance of Practicing

The final and most important factor in oral interpretation preparation is practice. This one step cannot be emphasized enough. Nothing is more obvious to an audience than an unprepared, unpolished oral reading. Very few people possess the reading skills necessary to provide a successful delivery without ample practice. You will want to concentrate on a variety of vocal changes as you practice. This includes changes in rate, volume, inflection, pitch and vocal quality. Correct pronunciation and articulation are essential if the audience is to understand the literature. Use emphasis to stress certain words without disturbing the author's original rhythm. An expressive voice will communicate meaning and insight into your reading.

Body Movements

Body movement can offer further understanding into the literature. You can do this through eye contact, facial expressions and gestures. You want all gesturing to be natural to enhance your performance. Remember to place the characters with your eye focus. The eye and head movement should be smooth and subtle — never awkward and excessive. You do not use large, overdone body movements, but you may add slightly exaggerated facial expressions to communicate meaning.

Handling Your Manuscript

Pay careful attention to the handling of your manuscript. It is advisable to put the manuscript in a folder for easier handling during the performance. A script which is typed with double-spaced lines will be easier to read and allows for space to mark the manuscript. Pages should be arranged in your folder so that you won't turn pages in the middle of a paragraph or verse of poetry. You want the audience to focus on you and the literature, not the distraction of your manuscript handling.

Practice your entire selection to ensure a smooth and natural performance. You may use a tape recorder to evaluate your vocal progress as you practice. A small group of friends serving as a rehearsal audience can be a valuable way of receiving feedback as you continue to polish your oral interpretation. Keep in mind that the oral interpretation performance of literature is for the entertainment and enlightenment of the audience. With this concept in mind, you will have a rewarding and enjoyable experience.

ACTIVITY — Oral Interpretation

OBJECTIVES

1. To develop reading skills through oral interpretation.
2. To foster an interest in different types of literature.

INSTRUCTIONS

1. Select literature, either prose or poetry, which you enjoy. Consider your audience when making your selection.

2. Take time analyzing the literature.

3. Cut your selection or combine selections to meet the time limit requirements. Time it several times as you practice.

4. Mark your manuscript to help express your interpretation of the literature during the performance.

5. Be sure you know the meaning and pronunciation of unfamiliar words. Look them up to be sure.

6. Prepare an introduction which includes author information, the title of the selection and an explanation of the literature.

7. Practice your selection several times. You are not simply reading your literature. You are interpreting it.

8. Place characters, if necessary. Create distinguishable voices for all characters.

9. Gestures, facial expressions, eye contact and body movement should be used appropriately. You are not acting, don't overdo it.

10. Vocal variety should be used. Vary the rate, volume, pitch and inflection. Be sure to articulate!

11. Have others evaluate your performance. You may use the suggested checklist.

Checklist for Good Oral Interpretation

1. Did the reader have an appropriate introduction?
2. Did the reader show insight into the literature?
3. Did the reader have good eye contact?
4. Did the reader have distinguishable characters?
5. Did the reader have natural and appropriate gestures?
6. Did the reader have exaggerated facial expressions?
7. Did the reader handle the manuscript well?
8. Did the reader bring the literature to life?

Readers Theatre

Oral reading is one of the best ways to feel the full meaning of literature. **Readers theatre** is a form of oral reading where a group of two or more readers present a piece of literature through vocal and physical suggestions. The action does not take place on stage, but rather in the minds of the audience. In readers theatre, oral readers use their voices and bodies to present literature in a dramatic form. This group interpretation is not acting, as in a play, but the speakers do suggest the characters by using their voices, facial expression and body movement. There are many kinds of literature which can be creatively and successfully used in readers theatre. Poetry, plays, and Bible readings are all used exceptionally well in readers theatre.

There are certain guidelines which will give you direction as you plan and perform your group oral interpretation. Scenery and costumes are rarely used and are only implied or suggested through the reader's creative use of voice and body movements. *Suggestion* is the way a speaker goes about creating the action, props, characters and scenery in the audience's imagination. You do not become the characters in the play, poem or story. You simply suggest them.

Movement should be limited, although some pantomime may be used to enhance the overall performance. Many readers theatre presentations arrange the readers in a formal formation on stage. The oral readers are sometimes arranged in a semicircle, seated on stools, facing the audience. Any type of simple stage arrangement can be used, as long as it is appropriate for the selection, audience and occasion.

The performers usually hold the scripts in hand as they perform, but in certain instances the scripts can be memorized. If scripts are used, they are put in dark colored folders for easier handling without distractions. Speakers rarely enter and exit from the stage area. The speakers remain on stage; and when no longer needed for the scene, they bow their heads or turn their backs to the audience, indicating they have left the scene or are no longer involved. Focus is generally off-stage toward the audience, although a particular scene may warrant on-stage eye contact between two characters. A narrator is commonly used to add lines which are needed to fill-in-the-blanks in the literature.

Options for Enhancing the Staging

Simple costumes and props, such as hats or shirts, are used to suggest the overall look desired. Sound effects and music may be incorporated into the performance, and spotlights may be used in the stage production for dramatic flair. Above all, technical additions to the oral reading should not interfere with the audience's use of imagination.

Selecting Pieces From Literature

When choosing literature for readers theatre, you need to decide if you will use several short pieces of literature combined, a single work which meets the time limit, or a cutting from a full-length work. Look for interesting characters, a strong theme and expressive language. Remember, as you select material for your readers theatre presentation to choose material which works well for a group reading. The literature will be divided between several readers, with each person using a script. The readers should speak clearly and put energy into every line.

Readers theatre enables oral readers to develop good performance skills, literary awareness, literature analysis skills and interpersonal communication through group work. What an exciting approach to the performance of literature!

ACTIVITY — Readers Theatre

OBJECTIVES

1. To develop good performance skills.
2. To develop literary awareness.
3. To develop interpersonal communication skills as you plan and perform the readers theatre.

INSTRUCTIONS

1. Get into groups of two to six people.
2. Discuss within your group the type of literature you would like to perform.
3. Choose material which is suitable for readers theatre.
4. Analyze the literature. Cut or combine selections.
5. Create a script from the literature selected.

---

6. Assign parts.

7. Stage the readers theatre presentation, deciding on movement, stage formation, costumes, character turns, lights and props. Remember to leave room for action in the imagination of the audience.

8. Rehearse and polish. Pay attention to cues and timing.

9. Perform for an audience.

10. Use vocal variety. Articulate!

11. Eye contact, gestures and facial expressions should be appropriate for the material.

12. Express the emotions, attitudes and actions of the characters by using vocal and physical clues to suggest the meaning.

Pet Cobwebs

Here is an example of a partial readers theatre script. This excerpt is taken from the book of children's poetry, *Pet Cobwebs*.

Speakers 1-5	Please
Speakers 1-5	Please
	Don't tease
	The bees!
Speaker 1	I might freeze
Speaker 2	Or flap my knees,
Speaker 3	Try to kiss Louise,
Speaker 4	Sail all seven seas,
Speaker 5	Get attacked by fleas,
Speaker 1	Be forced to eat peas,
Speaker 2	Turn into green cheese,
Speaker 3	Grab the toothpaste and squeeze,
Speaker 4	Become allergic and wheeze,
Speaker 5	Get a terrible disease,
Speaker 1	Start to speak Japanese,
Speaker 2	Blow away in the breeze,
Speaker 3	Or try to climb trees,

Speaker 4	Swing from a trapeze,
Speaker 5	I might even sneeze.
Speakers 1-5	Please
	Don't tease
	The bees!

Choral Reading

Another type of group interpretation which allows for creative group work is choral reading. It involves speakers combining their individual voices to speak in unison. It is not as simple as saying the same word at the same time. As with oral interpretation and readers theatre, choral speaking re-creates literature in a live performance. The audience is allowed to experience the literature as the readers give meaning to the printed word. Choral readers hold their scripts in the same way choir members hold their music.

Considerations for Selecting Choral Readings

You must analyze and select literature for your group presentation. Choose something simple for your first choral speaking experience. A prominent theme, strong rhythm and choice of script pattern are important considerations in making a selection. There are many wonderful styles of literature which can be successfully performed for choral reading. A strong rhythm in the literature helps the speakers stay synchronized. The theme must be easily identifiable and have universal appeal. Choral speaking should not be hard to understand if the audience is to get involved and enjoy the performance.

The group process requires cooperation, practice and teamwork. Exact pronunciation, articulation and timing are essential in choral speaking. Being a fraction of a second ahead or behind the other speakers will destroy the crisp, clear sound that is to be produced in a choral presentation. Much practice is needed to achieve a polished performance.

Script Patterns

Dividing the speakers' parts can be done in a number of ways. Script patterns can be done in complete unison of voices where all speakers recite the lines of the literature together, or where each speaker reads

127

one line until the cutting is complete. Another method adds speakers as lines are added. Speaker one says the first line; and speakers one and two say the second line; and so on, until the entire choral group speaks together. Another script pattern has two groups taking turns responding to one another. Group one says a line, and group two follows with a response. Several speakers may speak individually, and then all choral speakers could join in. A refrain can be created using an outstanding line in the literature. The entire group can recite these lines periodically throughout the choral reading. There are so many interesting ways to create different sounds and effects with inventive script patterns.

Presentation Disciplines

All speakers use the same type of folder to hold their scripts. Being in unison physically as well as vocally will greatly add to the overall effect. Speakers should know the lines well enough to briefly glance at their scripts for cues and lead lines. Opening and closing folders should also take place in unison. Memorization is allowable if it is appropriate for the literature and occasion. The choral speakers stand or use stools as they face the audience during the performance. Choral speakers may perform movement as a group, such as pointing or looking in a certain direction. Children's productions require more movement to entertain the audience members. As with readers theatre, your group interpretation may require new ideas and experimentation. Explore, create and have fun!

ACTIVITY — Choral Reading

O B J E C T I V E S

1. To develop good performance skills.
2. To develop literary awareness.
3. To develop interpersonal communication skills as you plan and perform choral reading.

I N S T R U C T I O N S

1. Get into groups of three to six people. Group size may vary, depending on the size of the overall group.
2. Choose literature which will be appropriate for choral speaking.
3. Analyze the literature. Cut or combine selections.

---

4. Select a script pattern or combine several script patterns to create an interesting choral reading.

5. Assign parts.

6. Stage the choral reading (movement, stage formation, costumes, lights, props).

7. Rehearse and polish.

8. Perform for an audience.

9. Use unison speaking for a portion of the presentation.

10. Character voices should be consistent throughout the presentation.

11. Use vocal variety.

12. Use unison movement, when appropriate.

13. Use eye contact and exaggerated facial expressions.

14. Speakers should enter and exit in unison.

Tongue Twisters

The articulators — teeth, tongue, lips, jaw, hard and soft palates — definitely need to be exercised in order to be ready for the oral reading experience. The last activity in this chapter is a collection of tongue twisters which can be used to promote good articulation and be a great deal of fun. Good luck with keeping your tongue untied!

"PETER PIPER PICKED..."

ACTIVITY — Tongue Twisters

OBJECTIVE

1. To develop articulation skills.

INSTRUCTIONS

1. Each person receives a copy of the tongue twisters.
2. One at a time each class member attempts as many tongue twisters as possible.
3. Keep score of how many tongue twisters you are able to read without mistakes.
4. Open your mouth as you clearly and carefully pronounce each word.

Tongue Twisters

1. A tutor who tooted the flute
   Tried to tutor two tutors to toot.
   Said the two to the tutor,
   "Is it harder to toot,
   Or to tutor two tutors to toot?"
2. Each sixth chick sat on a stick.
3. Six slim slick sycamore saplings.
4. Listen to the local vocal yokel yodel.
5. The big baby buggy with the red rubber buggy bumpers.
6. Rubber baby buggy bumpers
   Rubber baby buggy bumpers
   Rubber baby buggy bumpers.
7. "Lift the ladder later," lisped Lester.
   Lester lisped, "Lift the ladder later."
8. Peter Piper picked a peck of pickled peppers.
   A peck of pickled peppers Peter Piper picked.
   If Peter Piper picked a peck of pickled peppers,
   Where's the peck of pickled peppers Peter Piper picked?
9. An old scold sold a cold coal shovel.
10. Rush the washing, Russell
    Rush the washing, Russell
    Rush the washing, Russell.

11. Buy a black-backed bath brush.

12. I stood on the steps of Burgesses fish sauce shop
    Mimicking him hiccupping and welcoming him in.

13. The boot black brought the black boot back.

14. Lilly ladled little Letty's lentil soup.

15. Does your sport shop stock short socks with spots?

16. Moses supposes his toeses are roses,
    But Moses supposes erroneously,
    For nobody's toeses are posies of roses
    As Moses supposes his toeses to be.

17. Amos Ames, the amiable astronaut aided in an aerial
    enterprise at the age of eighty-eight.

18. Eat fresh fried fish free at the fish fry.

19. Tom threw Tim three thumbtacks.
    Three thumbtacks were thrown to Tim by Tom.
    Why did Tom throw Tim three thumbtacks?

20. I bought a box of biscuits
    A box of mixed biscuits and a biscuit mixer.

21. Three gray geese in the green grass, grazing.
    Gray were the geese and green was the grass
    In which the geese were grazing.

22. Frivolous fat Fanny fried fresh fish furiously
    Friday forenoon for four famished Frenchmen.

23. Of all the saws I ever saw saw, I never saw a saw saw
    like that saw saws.

24. A skunk sat on a stump.
    The stump thunk the skunk stunk.
    The skunk thunk the stump stunk.

25. Theophilus, the thistle sifter,
    While sifting a sifter full of thistles,
    Thrust three thousand thistles through the thick of his thumb.

26. Betty Botter bought some butter.
    "But," she said, "The butter's bitter.
    If I put it in my batter,

It will make my batter better."
So, she bought a bit of butter
And she put it in her batter and
It made her batter better.

27. How much wood would a woodchuck chuck
   If a woodchuck could chuck wood?

28. She sells seashells by the seashore.

29. A proper cup of coffee from a copper coffeepot.

30. Sinful Caesar sipped his snifter, seized his knees and sneezed.

31. Much whirling water makes the mill wheel work well.

CHAPTER TEN

Grab Bag
Variety of Speech Activities

Terms to Learn

diaphragm
resonators
pet peeve

There are many times when a new activity is needed to reinforce a lesson or idea being taught. A creative and stimulating project can provide an opportunity to apply the knowledge you have acquired from other speaking situations. This chapter offers a grab bag of various speech communications activities which will help you gain valuable speaking experience.

Twenty-Four Hour Silence

The first activity stresses the importance of speech communication. You will discover just how difficult everyday life would be without speech. At first thought, this assignment seems impossible; but with much self-control, concentration, and determination, you can learn to communicate with other means of communication. You can communicate through nonverbal communication. Sign language and gesturing can work to express many ideas you need to communicate. Written language may take time, but can successfully reveal any thoughts you wish to convey. Twenty-four hours without using speech to communicate is definitely challenging. The

133

importance of speech and the purposes for speaking become very apparent through this interesting assignment.

ACTIVITY — Twenty-Four-Hour Silence

O B J E C T I V E S

1. To demonstrate the importance of speech communication.
2. To emphasize the importance of nonverbal communication.

I N S T R U C T I O N S

1. Give each student a hand-out to fill out with the following information: (Adapt this hand-out to your schedule.)

> Teachers,
>
> _____ is participating in an optional speech assignment in which he/she will not speak for 24 hours. Sign language and written communication may be used, but whispering is not allowed. I hope this will not create a problem in your class today. If so, please exempt this student by signing the correct class period space. The student may, of course, participate in choir, athletics or band. There should be no speech, other than that which is absolutely necessary to be able to function in your particular class. Please sign if this student is successful during your class period. Thank you for your help and cooperation.
>
> ### *The Speech Department*
>
> **Teacher**   **Comments**
>
> 1st period _____
>
> 2nd period _____
>
> 3rd period _____
>
> 4th period _____
>
> 5th period _____
>
> 6th period _____

134

Homeroom _____

Parents   **Comments**

At home _____

2. Present the hand-out to your teacher upon entering the classroom. This will eliminate potential problems.

3. Don't abuse the right to use sign language and written communication. Use these forms of communication *only* when necessary.

4. Sounds such as clearing the throat, laughing, coughing and grunting are to be avoided, if possible.

5. Be on your honor as to whether or not you are successful. The activity is extremely difficult, so don't worry if you don't succeed. Hopefully, you will learn something beneficial from it and have fun trying.

6. The assignment works well if you begin as the speech class period ends. The silence begins as you leave the speech class. The 24 hours will end the following day during speech class. For example, if you have speech 2nd period, the assignment begins as you leave class 2nd period on Tuesday and is completed at the end of 2nd period on Wednesday.

7. The following day the participants can complete the assignment with a written or oral evaluation of what occurred and how they responded.

Positive Feedback

Learning to be positive in even the most negative, frustrating situations can prove to be very valuable and rewarding. Remarkable changes can take place by simply improving your attitude. Hopefully, this new attitude will bring about positive feedback. When you are positive, it is natural for others to respond positively.

ACTIVITY — Positive Feedback

O B J E C T I V E

1. To emphasize the importance of presenting a positive attitude.

I N S T R U C T I O N S

1. Choose one of your classes and concentrate on being as positive as possible for five class periods, five days consecutively.

2. Look at the teacher when she/he speaks.

3. Respond when you understand. This may be done orally or nonverbally with a smile or a nod.

4. Raise your hand and politely ask pertinent questions.

5. Use good posture. Be attentive.

6. Answer questions politely.

7. Greet the teacher, or exchange dialog at some time during the class period, if time allows.

8. Don't "apple polish" or act phony with your improved attitude. Be sincere.

9. Be on time to class.

10. Have class assignments prepared on time.

11. Follow all class rules.

12. Keep a daily diary. Record what you do and say; also, how the teacher responds.

13. At the end of the week, report the results. This may be done through an oral discussion or a written summation.

14. Do this assignment Monday through Friday. Try your very best to bring about a positive reaction from your teacher.

15. You may see such wonderful results from your positive attitude that you decide to continue the upbeat, favorable activity throughout the year.

16. You may also wish to try the same activity with your parents or a friend.

Diaphragmatic Breathing

A "filler" assignment which is a quick lesson in sustained breathing is an extremely important activity for speech and drama students. The proper use of the **diaphragm**, the large muscle at the bottom of the rib cage, allows you to control your breathing. Speech sounds are produced as you push air through the lungs with certain rib muscles and the diaphragm. The vocal folds in the larynx vibrate as the air is exhaled. The **resonators**, the bones and sinus cavities in your nose, throat and mouth, amplify the vocal sounds. Speech is produced as the articulators, the tongue, jaw, lips, teeth, hard and soft palates, mold the sounds and form words.

To be able to control airflow when speaking properly, you must learn to speak from the diaphragm. You can check for diaphragmatic breathing by placing a book on your diaphragm as you lie flat on your back. The book should be placed between the lower abdominal and chest areas, just above the waist. The book should rise as you inhale and fall as you exhale. Here's another activity which allows you a chance to practice control of your breathing. You inhale deeply and exhale as you produce the "oo" or "ah" vowel sounds. Work to sustain the vowel sound for as long as you can without allowing your voice to sound breathy or forced.

ACTIVITY — Diaphragmatic Breathing

O B J E C T I V E
1. To demonstrate the importance of breathing from the diaphragm.

I N S T R U C T I O N S

1. Each person should select one page from a textbook.
2. Each person should stand in front of the class and read as much of the

137

textbook selection as possible, while using a single breath.

3. The speaker's words should be understood and heard by all class members.

4. If the class would like to turn the exercise into a contest, a timer could be used to determine which class member can sustain his/her breath for the longest time, OR, all class members could read the same material to determine the winner.

The Speech to Entertain

The next activity entertains the audience through the use of humor. It is difficult to be humorous. Choice of an appropriate subject and choice of the right words is of utmost importance when adding humor to a speech to entertain. This type of speech is not merely a series of jokes or stories which are unconnected. The anecdotes and humorous illustrations should have a connecting link to the general theme of the subject. Use your own personality as you speak from personal interest, experience or knowledge. Your task to successfully entertain your audience will be much easier if you let your natural personality shine for your audience.

ACTIVITY — The Speech to Entertain

O B J E C T I V E

1. To promote self-confidence in speech making by using humor in a speech to entertain.

I N S T R U C T I O N S

1. Choose a main idea or theme for your speech to entertain.

2. Choose a subject which is appropriate for the situation.

3. Use several funny stories or anecdotes as illustrations. They must apply to the theme of the speech.

4. Experiment by using several different methods to achieve humor.

5. Organize your speech with an introduction, body and conclusion.

6. Select your material and arrange it so that it entertains your audience.
7. Delivery should be light and lively.
8. Hold for laughs from the audience, when necessary.
9. Time for the speech is three to five minutes.

Methods to Achieve Humor

1. use audience member's name in a joke
2. tell a joke about yourself
3. exaggerate lines or gestures
4. use surprise
5. use after-thoughts or asides
6. restate a cliché or quotation with your own personal touch added
7. facial expressions
8. impersonations
9. pantomime
10. clever wording
11. amusing examples
12. recent happenings in the news which could be humorous

Topic Suggestions

1. hospital experiences
2. dating
3. back-seat drivers
4. dreams
5. children
6. pets
7. how to raise your parents
8. learning to drive
9. dinner guests
10. habits

Statue Game

Learning to be expressive as an actor or speaker takes much practice. You want your listeners to correctly interpret the message you are sending. Nonverbal communication plays a vital role in our lives as communicators. The statue game is an excellent exercise which lets the actor demonstrate many different emotions through facial expressions and body positions.

ACTIVITY — Statue Game

OBJECTIVE

1. To encourage meaningful facial expressions and body movements.

INSTRUCTIONS

1. Divide into groups of four or five people.

2. One group will go to the stage area.

3. When a word is called, each group member, without looking at other group members, will freeze in a physical pose which expresses the emotional meaning of the given word.

4. The freeze must last for ten seconds.

5. The class members should notice the differences and similarities of all participants.

6. Each group will take a turn on stage.

List of Emotions

1. fear	6. sadness
2. joy	7. arrogance
3. courage	8. pain
4. surprise	9. jealousy
5. shyness	10. frustration

Nonsense Syllable Speaking

Talking in nonsense syllables is a fun way to communicate vocally without using real words. When you combine it with exaggerated body movement, it becomes a worthwhile exercise for creative improvisation as you invent the "new language" as you go. Adding another person with the nonsense syllables and body movement to create a scene allows for speech students to get practice in interactive expression. You learn to use your voice and body to convey an idea in a new and interesting way.

ACTIVITY — Nonsense Syllable Speaking

OBJECTIVE

1. To promote vocal and physical expressiveness through the nonsense syllable speaking exercise.

INSTRUCTIONS

1. Get into pairs.

2. Choose a scene idea which works well for two people.

3. The scene should be one which allows both actors to be very expressive, both vocally and physically.

4. By using nonsense syllables, communicate with the other actor on stage.

5. Both actors should interact with each other in complete understanding.

6. The nonsense language should be a combination of many speech sounds. Be careful not to use real words.

7. Use facial expressions, gesturing, good stage movement and vocal variety as you express yourself in your scene.

8. Create an understandable ending. Don't end abruptly. Leave the audience with a clear understanding of what took place.

Mock Trial

There are many situations which work well for improvisational theatre, some humorous, some serious. A murder trial would certainly be a dramatic challenge for improvisational actors. The entire class could participate in the mock trial.

ACTIVITY — Mock Trial

O B J E C T I V E S

1. To develop improvisational acting skills through the presentation of a mock trial.
2. To stimulate the decision-making process as important choices are made in the trial.

INSTRUCTIONS

1. Hold a mock trial. Set up a situation. Use the one which follows, or create one of your own.

2. Class members will play the parts of lawyers, witnesses, jury members and judge.

3. This is a re-enactment of a murder trial. Actors should be serious.

4. Create a distinctive character, no matter what character you play. Create mannerisms, vocal characteristics, posture and facial expressions to add to your character development.

5. Assign all parts.

6. Set the stage to resemble a courtroom.

Possible Trial Situation

A man or woman is accused of murder. The district attorney has evidence and witnesses. He is convinced of the defendant's guilt. The defense lawyer has witnesses and evidence, as well. He strongly believes in the defendant's innocence. There is no way to determine the jury's decision until the trial takes place. The judge should preside over business in the court. The lawyers should try to have a plan or direction as they continue to build their cases. The jury members should react to all evidence presented.

Television News

The next activity is a valuable activity because of the number of skills which can be developed through the course of the assignment. Writing, researching, interviewing and speaking are used to create a television news report. This assignment gives you the opportunity to see what it would be like to work as a member of a news team. Who knows? You might just decide to pursue television journalism as a profession!

ACTIVITY — Television News

O B J E C T I V E S

1. To develop self-confidence while delivering a television news speech.
2. To develop writing, researching, interviewing and speaking skills through preparation and presentation of the television news speech.

INSTRUCTIONS

1. Divide into groups of four people.
2. Assign news coverage assignments. Two people will handle news features; one will cover the weather; and one will report the sports.
3. Work as a group to prepare all news reports. Compile stories together.
4. Try to be entertaining and informative.
5. Present stories to the audience using the manuscript delivery.
6. Use visual aids such as maps, chalkboards, pictures, etc.
7. News coverage can be limited to school news or it could include local,

national or international features.

8. Time limit is eight to ten minutes.

Prominent Person Speech

A research speech which deals with a prominent contemporary person could be a good follow-up assignment for the chapter on researched speeches. There are many noteworthy individuals who would make excellent speech topics.

ACTIVITY — Prominent Person Speech

O B J E C T I V E S

1. To promote self-confidence in speech making in a prominent person speech.
2. To promote the use of research in speech writing.

I N S T R U C T I O N S

1. Write a speech about a prominent, contemporary person. Choose someone of interest to you.
2. The speech should contain several sources of material.
3. Try to give interesting information about the person you choose.
4. Organize your speech with an introduction, body and conclusion.
5. Time limit is two to three minutes.

The Human Interest Speech

Similar to the speech about a prominent person, but with a more personal tone, is the human interest speech. You have no doubt met many interesting and memorable people in your lifetime. Choose the one, *most* interesting person and write a speech about his/her life, personality and remarkable character traits.

ACTIVITY — The Human Interest Speech

O B J E C T I V E

1. To promote self-confidence in speech making in a human interest speech.

I N S T R U C T I O N S

1. Write a speech about the most interesting character you have ever known.

2. Describe the character's likable qualities. Tell about his/her personality strengths.

3. Recall specific details and incidents which further demonstrate the person's commendable qualities.

4. The speech should be personal and real.

5. Show friendliness, humanness and warmth.

6. Organize the speech with an introduction, body and conclusion.

7. Time limit is three to four minutes.

The Pet Peeve Speech

A speech which encourages you to express your frustration and anger is the *pet peeve* speech. A pet peeve is anything which upsets you — a thing which causes you anger. It is an act or occurrence which causes you stronger feelings than anything else. Your greatest pet peeve drives you crazy! When you speak about it, your blood begins to boil from the mere mention of it. This speech will allow you to display great emotion, both vocally and physically.

ACTIVITY — The Pet Peeve Speech

O B J E C T I V E

1. To encourage expression of emotions through the delivery of a pet peeve speech.

I N S T R U C T I O N S

1. Write a speech about your pet peeve.

2. Choose a topic about which you feel very strongly.

3. Express your personal feelings about the topic.

4. Use plenty of force as you express your emotions.

5. Organize your speech with an introduction, body and conclusion.

6. Use description and detail as you describe your greatest pet peeve.

7. Go "all out" vocally and emotionally.

8. Use strong, expressive gestures and facial expressions.

9. Your own feelings will be the source of your speech.

10. Time limit is one minute. Short, but powerful.

Topic Suggestions

1. people who bite their fingernails
2. someone scratching the chalkboard
3. someone chewing gum, or food, with an open mouth
4. people who constantly interrupt
5. knuckle poppers
6. people who don't properly care for their animals
7. hypocrites
8. people who are always late
9. being put on hold on the telephone
10. the dentist
11. slow drivers
12. procrastinators
13. sloppy people
14. people who constantly complain
15. people who borrow things without asking

Developing Listening Skills

An entire chapter could be devoted to the topic of listening. There are many worthwhile activities which can prepare you for being a better listener; simple activites, such as naming all sounds you love to hear. This exercise can be done in groups or individually. Another "filler" assignment has you list all sounds you hear for five minutes. You could list five phrases you like to hear someone say to you or compile a list of all the things which interfere with listening. As you study listening skills, you may choose to do one short activity every day. Use them as warm-up activities before you begin the lesson. Follow each listening activity with a short discussion which can give everyone in class a chance to share their ideas with the other students.

Story Recall

A listening activity which emphasizes listening for information is story recall. You must listen for details as you create a complete picture in your mind of what is being said. Listen for key words and main ideas. Try to concentrate on what the speaker is saying; let it sink in. It is a fun exercise which really tests your ability to listen carefully and recall what you have heard.

ACTIVITY — Story Recall

O B J E C T I V E

1. To promote good listening skills.

I N S T R U C T I O N S

1. Five people are selected from the entire group.

2. Four people leave the room, and one person remains in the room with the audience. The four people should not be able to hear what is being said in the room.

3. The instructor or leader reads a story aloud to the entire group.

4. Person number two is brought back into the room.

5. Person number one re-tells the same story to person number two. Person one tries to recall and re-tell the story as accurately as possible.

---

6. Person number three is brought back into the room. Person two now tells the story, as he/she heard it, to person number three.
7. Person four is brought in to hear the story from person three.
8. Person five is brought in to hear the story from person four.
9. Person five tells the story to the audience.
10. Each person should tell the story, as closely as possible, the way it was told to him/her.

One important point to make about this activity is that people don't intentionally change the story. Everyone hears the story in a unique way as it relates to him/her personally. Gossip takes the same basic course as the details in the stories. Important facts and details are changed from person to person. After five people have heard and repeated a story, the story no longer resembles the original version at all. It's amazing to see how much the story changes.

Story One

(Listen carefully as I read you a story about an automobile accident.)

Last Thursday night at 9:02 p.m., it was raining very hard. The traffic in Dallas was piling up everywhere. Twenty-nine accidents had already been recorded in the city. On the corner of Oak and 42nd Avenue, near the Burger King Restaurant, an accident occurred. The driver of a black Camaro failed to use his turn signal and was sideswiped by a red Volkswagen. There were three people in the red car and two people in the Camaro. The driver of the Camaro was not hurt except for a busted lip. The boy driving the Volkswagen broke his arm. The others in both cars received only minor injuries. Officer Westfall arrived at the scene of the accident and issued Tom Jenkins, the driver of the black Camaro, a citation for failure to use his turn signal. Bill Foreman also received a ticket for speeding. He was going 45 miles per hour in a 30 mph zone. The metropolitan ambulance arrived and took the drivers of both cars to

Southwest Methodist Hospital in downtown Dallas. Tom Jenkins received stitches above his lip, and Bill Foreman got a cast on his arm.

Story Two

(Listen carefully as I read you a story about a rescue on a beach.)

As we were standing on the edge of the beach on Silver Lake, which is located just outside of Willow Creek, Alabama, something strange happened. It was shortly after noon on March 25th, because we had heard the noon bell from a local church only minutes before.

A young boy about nine years old was fishing from a rowboat. His line began to jerk fiercely as he stood up to reel in a mighty big catch. As he started to get the fish with a net a motorboat with a skier roared by. The skier's wake rolled up against the rowboat, knocking the boy and fish into the water.

A big Brittany spaniel swam toward the boy and grabbed him by the collar of his jacket. The boy and dog made it safely back to shore, and the motorboat disappeared around a bend in the lake.

Story Three

(Listen carefully as I read you a story about a tornado.)

On July 15th, it was a very hot and dry day in Seminole, Texas. We were sitting on the back patio of our house trying to cool off. It was late in the afternoon when we noticed the sky turning blackish-gray. A few minutes later, we saw funnel-shaped clouds coming from the southwest.

We knew that they were tornado clouds, so we went to the basement for shelter. Through the basement window, we saw a pick-up truck lifted up by the wind and set down on top of Moses Brothers' Department Store. On the opposite side of the street, all of the windows were broken and the doors ripped off the hinges.

Later, we found out that many stores, like the hardware store, had their interiors destroyed. Other stores were not damaged at all. In the ice cream store, the sugar cones were stacked in neat piles on the counter just behind the broken windows. On our side of the street, nothing was touched at all, except for a fire hydrant which was knocked over and spewing water like a fountain.

Story Four

(Listen carefully as I read you a story of a Yorkshire terrier's kidnapping.)

On September 12th, it was a warm, clear day in Dallas. We were all waiting in the Delta boarding lounge at the airport. Our 747 jet was scheduled to leave for Nashville in twenty minutes.

A black and tan Yorkshire terrier with a red bow in her hair was sitting on the lap of an elderly woman. Many people had stopped to pat the little dog on the head and ask the woman how the dog was going to travel aboard the airplane. She was explaining the airline's rules and the dog's black carrying case to a well-dressed man when a firecracker exploded about five feet away. The dog bolted into the crowd.

We saw a man in a black raincoat pick up the dog and run through the crowd into a room marked, "Employees Only." We watched until we had to board the plane. We never saw anyone enter or leave that room.

Story Five

(Listen carefully as I read you a story of a window cleaner's accident.)

It was early in the morning of March 16th, a bright, beautiful day. We had just arrived at work on the top floor of the old

Planter's Building in Philadelphia.

We saw a window cleaner who spent almost two hours setting up pulleys and a platform. He was finally ready to step out onto the platform and clean windows.

Thirty minutes later, we saw a gigantic purple balloon floating past the windows. The balloon looked about 50 feet tall. Hanging from the balloon was a wicker basket with a beautiful woman in it. The basket swung too close to the building, and appeared to knock the window cleaner off the platform. We all rushed to the window to see what had happened. The woman in the basket had grabbed the window cleaner, and his feet were kicking in midair. The balloon finally glided away from the building, and landed safely in a globe willow tree in the park across the street near the fountain.

Progress Report

As students progress through this course, it's important for them to take time to analyze their progress and personal growth. The teacher discovers just exactly what each student feels he/she has learned. This can be done periodically throughout the course. It is beneficial for both teacher and student as they evaluate the activities which have been especially worthwhile in accomplishing the course goals and objectives.

ACTIVITY — Progress Report

O B J E C T I V E

1. To evaluate the progress being made in the speech communications class.

I N S T R U C T I O N S

1. Write a paper about the progress you feel you have made in class.

2. Describe what you feel you have learned thus far in this class.

3. Tell which activities have been very beneficial to you personally.

4. Relate which exercises and assignments have been your favorites and why.

5. Length of the assignment should be three or four paragraphs.

151

Helpful Suggestions

One way to avoid problems in any speech topic selection is to use a sign-up sheet. Those who decide upon topic ideas sign up as soon as they make a selection.

No duplications of the topic are allowed. For example, if John chooses the basketball for his object speech, no other class member will be allowed to do an object speech on the basketball. No two speakers speak on the same topic. There's no chance of copying ideas, and the variety of topics is much more interesting for the audience.

Those who decide first have the widest selection of topics. Those who are slower in choosing a topic must check the sign-up sheet to be sure their choice hasn't already been selected.

A sign-up sheet also provides the teacher with a written indicator of all speakers and their speech topics. It can be used very successfully for most speech assignments.

On the following page, a sample sign-up sheet is provided for your use. It can be duplicated on the copier at the same size or enlarged up to a maximum of 130% to fit on an 8½" x 11" piece of paper.

SIGN-UP SHEET

Type of Speech _____

Name   **Speech Topic**

Bibliography

Albright, Hardie. *Acting, The Creative Process.* Belmont, CA: Dickenson Publishing Company, Inc., 1969.

Breen, Robert S. *Chamber Theatre.* Englewood Cliffs, NJ: Prentice-Hall, Inc., 1978.

Brooks, William D. and Gustav W. Friedrich. *Teaching Speech Communication in the Secondary School.* Boston: Houghton Mifflin Company, 1973.

Buys, William E., Roy A. Beck, Martin Corbin, Paul Hunsinger, Melvin H. Miller and Robert L. Scott. *Creative Speaking.* Skokie, IL: National Textbook Company, 1974.

Carlile, Clark S. *38 Basic Speech Experiences.* Pocatello, ID: Clark Publishing Company, 1960.

Clark, Richard. *Effective Speech.* Encino, CA: Glencoe Publishing Co., Inc., 1982.

Coger, Leslie Irene and Melvin R. White. *Readers Theatre Handbook.* Glenview, IL: Scott, Foresman and Company, 1967.

Dietrich, John E. *Play Direction.* Englewood Cliffs, NJ: Prentice-Hall, Inc., 1953.

Galvin, Kathleen and Cassandra Book. *Person to Person, An Introduction to Speech Communication.* Skokie, IL: National Textbook Company, 1974.

Galvin, Kathleen M., Pamela J. Cooper and Jeannie McKinney Gordon. *The Basics of Speech.* Lincolnwood, IL: National Textbook Company, 1988.

Hedde, Wilhelmina G., William Norwood Brigance and Victor M. Powell. *The New American Speech.* Philadelphia: J. B. Lippincott Company, 1963.

Hopkins, Mary Francis and Beverly Whitaker. *Contemporary Speech.* Skokie, IL: National Textbook Company, 1976.

Lee, Charlotte and David Grote. *Theatre: Preparation and Performance.* Glenview, IL: Scott, Foresman and Co., 1982.

Long, Beverly Whitaker, Lee Hudson and Phillis Rienstra Jeffrey. *Group Performance of Literature.* Englewood Cliffs, NJ: Prentice-Hall, Inc., 1977.

Novelly, Maria C. *Theatre Games for Young Performers.* Colorado Springs, CO: Meriwether Publishing Ltd., 1985.

O'Connor, J. Regis. *Speech: Exploring Communication.* Englewood Cliffs, NJ: Prentice-Hall, Inc., 1988.

Owens, Fred. *Theatre Games.* Los Angeles, CA: Diamond Heights Publishing Company, Inc., 1975.

Prentice, Diana and James Payne. *More Than Talking: Analysis and Activities in Group Communication.* Caldwell, ID: Clark Publishing Company, 1983.

Schanker, Harry H. *The Spoken Word.* New York: McGraw-Hill Book Company, 1982.

Spolin, Viola. *Improvisation for the Theatre.* Evanston, IL: Northwestern University Press, 1972.

Tanner, Fran Averett. *Basic Drama Projects.* Pocatello, ID: Clark Publishing Company, 1972.

Tanner, Fran Averett. *Creative Communication.* Caldwell, ID: Clark Publishing Company, 1979.

Walker, Bonnie L. *Speech and Drama Activities for Secondary Students.* U.S.A.: Hayes School Publishing Company, Inc., 1984.

Wilkinson, Charles A. *Speaking of . . . Communication.* Glenview, IL: Scott, Foresman and Company, 1975.

Zorn, John W. *Speech for All.* Cambridge, MA: Educators Publishing Service.

About the Author

Carol Robinson Marrs is a wife, mother, teacher and writer. She received a degree in speech, drama and English education from West Texas State University and has taught junior high and high school students for 12 years. Her involvement in performance and competitive speech has contributed to many individual speaking awards won by her students, as well as many team trophies.

She was selected as an Outstanding Young Woman of America in 1986. She has been a member of professional organizations such as: Texas Association for the Improvement of Reading, PTA, Society of Children's Book Writers, American Association of Cheerleading Coaches and Advisors and "Just Say No" organization.

She wrote and self-published a book of children's poetry entitled, *Pet Cobwebs,* which her husband, Greg, illustrated. With brother, Dale, she co-produced an audio tape of poems and songs from *Pet Cobwebs*. She enjoys visiting local schools where she performs her poetry and songs for groups of students. Her writings also include skits, plays, short stories and greeting cards.

She and husband, Greg, have two children.

Notes

Notes

Order Form

Meriwether Publishing Ltd.
PO Box 7710
Colorado Springs, CO 80933-7710
Phone: 800-937-5297 Fax: 719-594-9916
Website: www.meriwether.com

Please send me the following books:

_____ **The Complete Book of Speech**   **$17.95**
Communication #BK-B142
by Carol Marrs
Ideas and activities for speech and theatre

_____ **Speechcraft #BK-B149**   **$17.95**
by Brent C. Oberg
An introduction to public speaking

_____ **Forensics #BK-B179**   **$17.95**
by Brent C. Oberg
The winner's guide to speech contests

_____ **Interpersonal Communication #BK-B260**   **$16.95**
by Brent C. Oberg
An introduction to human interaction

_____ **Two Character Plays for Student**   **$16.95**
Actors #BK-B174
by Robert Mauro
A collection of 15 one-act plays

_____ **Theatre Games for Young Performers**   **$16.95**
#BK-B188
by Maria C. Novelly
Improvisations and exercises for developing acting skills

_____ **112 Acting Games #BK-B277**   **$17.95**
by Gavin Levy
A comprehensive workbook of theatre games

These and other fine Meriwether Publishing books are available at your local bookstore or direct from the publisher. Prices subject to change without notice. Check our website or call for current prices.

Name: _____ e-mail: _____

Organization name: _____

Address: _____

City: _____ State: _____

Zip: _____ Phone: _____
❑ **Check enclosed**
❑ **Visa / MasterCard / Discover #** _____

Signature: _____ *Expiration date:* _____ / _____
     (required for credit card orders)

Colorado residents: Please add 3% sales tax.
Shipping: Include $3.95 for the first book and 75¢ for each additional book ordered.

❑ *Please send me a copy of your complete catalog of books and plays.*